SADDLES AND SPURS

The Pony Express Saga

SADDLES AND SPURS
The Pony Express Saga

Raymond W. Settle
Mary Lund Settle

UNIVERSITY OF NEBRASKA PRESS
Lincoln and London

International Standard Book Number 0–8032–5765–1

Library of Congress Catalog Card Number 55–10776

First Bison Book printing: October 1972

Most recent printing shown by first digit below:

6   7   8   9   10

Bison Book edition reproduced from the first (1955)
edition published by The Stackpole Company by
arrangement with Mary Lund Settle.

Manufactured in the United States of America

To our beloved daughters, PAULINE MARIE SHARP and MARILYN RAY BRICKER, whose womanly strength of character, confident self-reliance, and beautiful devotion to duty prove their spiritual kinship to the heroes mentioned herein, this volume is dedicated.

ERRATA

The following names of riders should be added to the Honor Roll on pages 74–76: Buck Cole, Bill Corbett, John Y. Denny, Alex Diffenbacher, J. Dodge, Gus Lashonse, Sam Litskey, and William M. Richards.

Page 42, line 3: *Read* 190 *for* 119

Page 95: *In picture caption read* Ismert *for* Jsmert

Page 106: *In photo credit read* Ismert *for* Jsmert

Page 119: *Line 3 should read:* Kennekuk, the first stage and fifth Pony Express relay station west

Page 163: *Credit should read:* From *The Pony Express.* Courtesy of Col. Waddell F. Smith

Page 183, line 11: *Read* R. M. and W. *for* R. M. and . . .

Page 190, line 11: *Read* 1864 *for* 1866

Page 190: *Last paragraph should read:* The Pony Express stopped on October 24, 1861, and Holladay took over the Central Overland California & Pike's Peak Express Company on March 2, 1862. The telegraph line was completed and the Pony Express officially came to an end. It appears, however, that a few more runs were made, possibly to clear the route of *mochilas* in transit.

Page 196, line 19: *Read* one third *for* one half

PREFACE

IN THE preparation of this volume the authors have labored to make a worthwhile contribution to the Pony Express saga. Simply another book on that subject never was their aim. Having collected much valuable information while doing research for a previous volume they felt that knowledge should be shared with others.

In order to fully accomplish this purpose they endeavored to project the story against the background of time, place, and interrelationships. It was therefore deemed necessary to include biographical sketches of the founders, company personnel, riders, and of the great overland mail issue, the freighting and stage coach business, the telegraph, and Pacific railroad.

In addition to all else, they also undertook to assemble a pictorial record of the Pony Express, something no one else appears to have done. With that in view they launched a nationwide search for photographs relating to the story. More than a thousand letters were written to individuals, libraries, museums, art galleries, commercial institutions, etc., thousands of pages of musty old newspapers were turned, and every book bearing directly or indirectly upon the subject was searched. The result was a collection of approximately three hundred photographs, some of the best of which appear in this volume.

In a work of this kind the services of a multitude of people were enlisted. Although it would be a pleasure to list the names of all of them, space limitations forbid. Among those who deserve special mention are Miss Louise Kampf, Coburn Library, Colorado Springs, Colorado; San Francisco Public Library; Denver Library; Virginia State Library, Richmond, Virginia; Library of Congress, Washington, D. C.; Kansas City Public Library, Kansas City, Missouri; New York City Public Library; Harold's Club, Reno, Nevada; Colonel Waddell F. Smith, San Rafael, California; ex-governor Charles R. Mabey, Bountiful, Utah; Miss Sarah Russell, Palmyra, Missouri; Dr. Ergo Majors, Oakland, California;

Morrell & Company, Topeka, Kansas; Mrs. John Wall, Sedalia, Missouri; Colorado State Historical Society, Denver Colorado; M. K. Goetz Brewing Company, St. Joseph, Missouri; St. Joseph Museum, St. Joseph; Elks Lodge, Denver; Los Angeles County Museum, Los Angeles; Chicago, Burlington & Quincy Railroad Company, National Park Service, Scotts Bluffs, Nebraska; Utah State Historical Society, Salt Lake City, Utah; M. E. Ismert, Kansas City; Leavenworth Public Library, Leavenworth, Kansas; Nebraska State Historical Society, Lincoln; Division of Resources and Development, Jefferson City, Missouri; Grand Central Art Galleries, New York; John Hancock Life Insurance Company, Boston; Home Insurance Company, New York; Bancroft Library, Berkeley, California; Library of the University of Wyoming, Laramie; Mrs. Nora McCaig, Dinubia, California; C. M. Ismert, Kansas City; Mrs. Minnie Fisher Ellsworth, Oakland; Paul Henderson, Alliance, Nebraska and American Air Lines.

Raymond W. Settle
Mary Lund Settle

Monte Vista, Colo.

CONTENTS

1

THE MEN WHO OPERATED
THE PONY EXPRESS

SINCE INSTITUTIONS are the lengthened shadows of men, brief sketches of those who boldly conceived and efficiently operated the Pony Express will not be out of place in the beginning of this story.

William H. Russell, whose name is most prominently associated with that romantic organization, was a lineal descendant of Lord William Russell, who lost his head on Lincoln's Inn Field, London, July 21, 1683, because of participation in the Rye-house plot against King Charles II. Almost a century later three descendants of his, David, Stephen, and Benjamin Russell, came to America. The latter settled in Vermont, where he married Betsy Ann Eaton. One of their eleven children, William Eaton, married Betsy Ann Hepburn, of the Scotland clan of that name. She did not live many years. Next he married her younger sister Myrtilla, who bore him two children, Adala Elizabeth and a son, William Hepburn, the latter known to history as William H., and hailed as the principal actor in the swiftly moving drama of the flying postman of the plains and mountains. He was born in Burlington, Vermont, January 31, 1812.

William Eaton Russell served in the War of 1812, is said to have been commander of the land forces in the diminutive, forgotten Battle of Lake Champlain, and died in 1814. On January 1, 1816, Mrs. Russell married Oliver Bangs, also a soldier in the War of 1812, and 2nd lieutenant in the 3rd United States Artillery, whose home was at Vergennes, Vermont.

Exactly when or why the family migrated to Western Missouri is not quite clear, but it was in the latter 1820s, for there is evidence that Bangs was connected with the Iowa Indian Agency in some manner in the early part of President Jackson's administration.

At that time young William H. was just past his middle 'teens. He went to work for Ely & Curtis, pioneer merchants in the frontier town of Liberty. His Yankee ideas, ways, and speech must have made him very conspicuous among the homely frontier people among whom he lived, but he got along very well.

Next he was employed by James Aull & Samuel Ringo of the same place. Aull was one of the famous trio of brothers who for many years exercised a profound influence over the Santa Fe and fur trade, and the business and economic life of Western Missouri. John and Robert were the others. They also operated stores in Independence, Richmond, and Lexington.

Some time in the early part of 1830 he was sent down the Missouri River to the busy, ambitious town of Lexington, which at that time surpassed any other in Western Missouri in trade, wealth, and prestige. It was both a retail and wholesale center for a wide area north and south of the river and a vigorous competitor with Westport for the Santa Fe and fur trade.

Like most young men of that region, place, and time, Russell's education was largely secured in the stern school of practical, everyday experience. He learned to spell well, used fairly good grammar, and wrote a passable hand early in life. In later years it degenerated into an almost indecipherable scrawl.

His training at Aulls, though severe, was admirably adapted to the needs of a young man of his talents and type. He was energetic, dependable, and keen on learning the business. His duties, which were multitudinous, covered a wide field of activity. He kept books, wrote letters in the office, collected bills, checked invoices of goods received by steamer, swept the floor of nights and made fires of mornings.

His relations here were pleasant and fortunate, for he had a rare opportunity to learn the frontier mercantile business from the ground up under the best of teachers.

On June 9, 1835, at twenty-three years of age, he married Harriet Elliot, daughter of the Reverend John Warder, who built his own church upon his own farm and preached whatever he pleased in it for many years. That alliance assured Russell of social recognition. Having established a family his next thought was to get in business for himself. He was getting along very well at Aulls, but knew he could get nowhere on a clerk's wages in those days.

In 1837 he made his first venture in helping to organize the Lexington First Addition Company and subscribed for five shares in it. It is interesting to note that William Bradford Waddell was also a member of this company and a stockholder in it. The following year Russell cut loose from his old employers and joined with James S. Allen and William Early to open a store under the name of Allen, Russell & Company.

In 1844 he formed a partnership with James H. Bullard to open another store which was called Bullard & Russell. Although the firm of Allen, Russell & Company failed in 1845, he apparently enjoyed a considerable degree of prosperity through this period. He bought town lots in Lexington and several thousand acres of rich Lafayette County farm lands. By the time he was in his middle thirties he was recognized as one of the up-and-coming young business men of the town and was eager to expand.

An opportunity to enter a new field came in 1847 when his firm of Bullard & Russell joined with E. C. McCarty, of Westport, to send a wagon train of merchant's goods from that place to Santa Fe. This venture in a business with which his name was to be associated forever afterward was evidently successful for they sent another train in 1848.

In 1849 he had his first experience freighting military supplies under contract with the government when he and James Brown sent a train down to Santa Fe. The next year they took in John S. Jones of Pettis County, Missouri, and under the name of Brown, Russell & Company delivered 600,000 pounds of military supplies in Santa Fe. Brown died in that city in December and the surviving partners carried on as Jones & Russell in 1851 and 1852. After the latter year the partnership was dissolved, but they were destined to work together in far greater undertakings in the days to come.

After Russell went into business for himself his advancement up the social and civic ladder in Lexington was rapid. He became a member of the Baptist church with his wife and was one of its main supporters. He adopted the extreme radical pro-slavery sentiments of the people among whom he lived. When the battle to make Kansas a slave state began in 1854 he threw himself into it with ardent enthusiasm. He was treasurer of the Lafayette County Emigration Society, an organization to assist pro-slavery settlers in the Territory, and was identified with Senator David R. Atchison's notorious Law and Order Party which seized control of the first Territorial Legislature.

With the coming of prosperity he built a twenty room mansion at the corner of South and 14th Streets on a large plot of ground, furnished it sumptuously according to the ideals of the day, laid out a formal garden in the rear, built a roomy stable and coach house, and kept the finest of horses. Across the street, a short block to the west, was the home of his old friend and associate, William B. Waddell.

By the time Russell was forty years of age he had attained outstanding success in every field. He possessed money, land, and an expansive domestic establishment, the prerequisites and passport to social eminence in the town. His ability as an organizer and promoter was conceded, his judgment and opinions carried much weight, and his seat among the mighty was secure. He stood at the forefront of every community movement, and his name was associated with every civic enterprise.

In 1850 he helped organize the Lexington Mutual Fire & Marine Insurance Company and served as director for many years. The people of the town thought they needed a "college" for their young women. He thought so too, and with Waddell, became one of the founders of the Lexington Female Collegiate Institute in 1851. It was not a success. Therefore in 1855 he and Waddell led a movement to take it over as a Baptist institution. This was done, and as such it existed until 1916.

In 1851 he became a member of the firm of Morehead, Waddell & Company. Morehead was his brother-in-law and Waddell was William B. About a year later Morehead retired and the name was changed to Waddell & Russell. In 1855 this firm was merged with a new co-partnership variously known as Majors & Russell and Russell, Majors & Waddell.

The rise of the young emigrant from the Granite State to a position of wealth and influence in a country and social enviroment to which, in many respects, he was a total stranger, presents all of the elements of an Horatio Alger romance. Although he was not a frontiersman in any sense, and bore the indelible marks of New England tradition and training to the end of his day, he possessed a remarkable degree of ability to adapt himself to the place and time in which he lived.

If Russell ever roughed it, or made a trip across the plains with one of his own wagon trains, no record of it exists. The idea, oft expressed, that he got his start in life walking along the dusty trail driving oxen is pure imagination. The first trip of record he ever made upon the plains was to Denver in 1861 upon the cushions of a Concord coach. He loved town and city life, luxurious living, and clean sheets upon his bed at night. An aged woman who spent some years of her girlhood in his Lexington home said that dinner every evening was a formal affair and that Russell always appeared dressed in spotless linen and decorous black suit.

From the very beginning Russell's business career was remarkable for breadth and variety of interests. Always, he was ready to go into anything that showed promise of profit. He has been characterized as "visionary," a "plunger" and even as a "gambler" by critics whose knowledge of him and the times in which he lived were incomplete and faulty. This is wholly unfair. Speculator he was, on a broad-gauge scale, like every other man on the frontier who had an extra dollar or could borrow one. Land was cheap, the country was filling up with settlers, business was booming, the West was being exploited, and the foundations for fortunes, some of which exist in and around Lexington to this day were being laid. The names of a dozen men in Lafayette County and scores of others elsewhere who were his counterparts, could be recorded. Some of them achieved wealth and hung onto it. Others, like Russell, got it only to lose it. If he deserves any of those harsh cognomens, so do they all.

That the business men and citizens of Lexington believed in Russell and highly respected him is quite obvious. His record for more than two decades was without spot or blemish. During that time he was regarded as one of the town's most progressive, solid citizens. Then, in the year 1860, in the far away city of Washington, he, by one act, stained that shining record. Anyone who studies his remarkable life, including this incident, turns from it

Courtesy of Dr. Ergo Majors and Col. Waddell Smith

Alexander Majors

all with a feeling of intense sadness that a brilliant career such as his should close under a shadow.

Alexander Majors' origin and background were totally unlike those of William H. Russell. He was born near Franklin, Kentucky, deep in the heart of the "Old South", October 4, 1814. Four years later his father, Benjamin, loaded the family into a covered wagon and set out for the farthest west frontier, Missouri. Crossing the Ohio River, probably at Louisville, they traveled across Southern Illinois and arrived upon the bank of the Mississippi River opposite St. Louis in the month of October, 1818. Here they were sent across the river in a ferry boat operated by three jolly French-Canadians. Proceeding on their way they crossed the Missouri River at St. Charles and plodded along the Boone's Lick Trail westward through mostly unsettled country. One evening when they were in camp for the night, the mother stepped upon the wagon tongue to get some cooking utensils. Her foot slipped, she fell, and sustained injuries from which she never recovered.

At the site of future Glasgow, Missouri, they crossed the Missouri River again, and spent the winter a few miles downstream in what was then known as "Cox's Bottom." Early in the spring of 1819 they again traveled westward along a route which would soon be known as the "Santa Fe Trail". They crossed Big Sni-A-Bar Creek some thirty miles below the mouth of the Kaw River and halted on what was known as the Fort Osage Military Reservation, where Benjamin erected a crude log shelter for his family. In 1820 the mother died from the effects of the fall from the wagon tongue.

It is significant that Alexander spent his boyhood and young manhood upon the newest frontier of the day. He became intimately acquainted with back-breaking toil in the clearing of land, splitting rails, erecting log cabins, and wrestling with the soil to produce a crop. Unlike Russell he was a typical frontiersman and remained such to the end of his days.

On November 6, 1834, he married Miss Catherine Stalcup of Jackson County, Missouri, who was in every way qualified to help build a frontier home. They moved to Cass County, settled upon a farm on the headwaters of Grand River, and proceeded to make a start in life. The work was hard, and with an increasing family of daughters a sense of futility began to grow within him. With a limited income from farming he felt he could not clothe and educate them as he should.

At length he decided to supplement that income by trading with the Indians who lived just west of the Missouri border. Loading a wagon with whatever he thought might please the partly civilized Pottawatomies, he drove to their reservation on the Kaw

River in the summer of 1846. On that trip he did a lot of thinking about freighting on the Santa Fe Trail. That was natural, for wagons had been rolling over it since 1822. In the spring of 1848 he got a contract from somebody to transport merchandise to Santa Fe, invested in six wagons, seventy or eighty oxen to draw them, and wrote out a pledge for his six bullwhackers to sign. It read:

"While I am in the employ of A. Majors, I agree not to use profane language, not to get drunk, not to gamble, nor to treat the animals cruelly, and not to do anything incompatible with the conduct of a gentleman. I agree if I violate any of the above conditions to accept my discharge without any pay for my services."

In writing that pledge and requiring his employees to sign and keep it, Majors was giving expression to his lifelong, stern, Calvinistic Presbyterian sentiments. He read his Bible regularly, attended church when he could, and sought to practice Christian principles in all his relations with other men.

Bullwhacking in that day was a rough mode of life and many of those who followed it were uncouth, profane individuals who believed that maximum service from the patient oxen was to be gotten only by swearing and a generous application of the whip. Majors did not want that kind of men working for him, and they didn't. There were men of the type he wanted to be had, men of high moral character who felt as Majors did. The other kind worked for sombody else. That there was much sound, common sense in employing the kind of men he wanted, none can deny.

His 1848 trip to Santa Fe, which began three months late on August 10, was made in ninety-two days, the quickest on record. In 1849 he again made the trip, and in 1850 he used ten wagons and about 130 oxen. Upon his return in the fall he learned that the quartermaster at Fort Leavenworth had twenty loads of supplies he wished to forward to Fort McKay on the Arkansas River near present Dodge City, Kansas. Although it was long past the time for starting, he took the contract, delivered the goods in first class condition, paused long enough to haul logs a distance of twenty-five miles to complete the Fort, and was back home before the winter storms descended upon the prairies. This was his first experience with military freighting. The contract he got in 1851 required twenty-five wagons and almost 300 oxen. In the spring of 1852 he sold his oxen to California emigrants, coralled his wagons, and remained at home.

When the year 1853 rolled around he bought new oxen and made another trip to Santa Fe with private goods. As in 1850 he made a second trip to Fort Union with military supplies including 100 wagons, 1200 oxen, and 120 men. This was a very good showing for a man who six years before had trudged his lonely way to the Pottawatomie Indian Reservation with one wagon and a dozen oxen. He had made money and could clothe and educate his daughters with the best of them.

Of all the men engaged in the freighting business in the latter 1850's none was better qualified for it in every way than Alexander Majors. All his life he had worked oxen in the forest, field, and on the road. He knew them from long intimacy, loved them, and held a high regard for them as living creatures. This knowledge and appreciation was highly important, for the manner in which they were handled under the yoke could go a long way toward determining the profit or loss on a freighting contract.

Majors was also highly successful in handling men on the trail, mainly because he himself was highly efficient in everything they were required to do. He had driven oxen day after day, cooked his own meals over a camp fire of cow-chips, slept under a wagon of nights from the Missouri River to Santa Fe, borne the searing heat of summer, and the numbing cold of winter. Even when his employees numbered into the thousands, every one of them respected and admired him, knew he perfectly understood their way of life, and cheerfully obeyed him. By training, inclination, and experience he was thoroughly adapted to captain the great squadrons of white topped Conestogas his firm later sent out upon the road.

In 1854 a new policy for supplying military posts west of the Missouri River was instituted. Who fathered the idea is not known. Under the old system, which had been in vogue since 1846 when such posts were few, the transportation of supplies for each was let to individuals or firms with small outfits hastily thrown together after the contract was signed. When the number of posts multiplied, this system was not satisfactory to either the government or contractors because plans for wagons, bull-whackers, and oxen could not be made in advance.

Somebody suggested that a single contract for the delivery of all supplies for all the posts be made with one firm or individual for two years. In other words, give somebody a monopoly. Competitive bidding was abandoned and the quartermaster at Fort Leavenworth was instructed to make a contract with someone financially able and qualified by experience to do the job. Since neither Majors, nor Russell and Waddell, were able to finance such a proposition alone they got together late in 1854 and formed the co-partnership which became effective January 1, 1855.

Waddell was of Scotch descent. His paternal grandfather, John was born in Glasgow in 1724. At eleven years of age he was apprenticed to a man by the name of Carter and brought to Fauquier County, Virginia, where he grew to manhood. In 1757 he married Elizabeth Green and is said to have fought in the Revolutionary War. His seventh child, also named John, was born in that County and married Catherine Bradford, a descendant of Governor William Bradford of Plymouth Colony. Their eldest son William Bradford, was born October 14, 1807. In 1811 the mother died, the father married Sarah Crow in 1813, and the family moved to Mason County, Kentucky in 1815.

This removal was highly important to young William Bradford, for at that time Mason County was on the high road to the West, by the Ohio River. Already the tide of emigrants which would add Missouri to the family of states was rapidly gaining momentum. Being situated as it was, the people living along it picked up information concerning both the East and the West. John Waddell, having emigrated once, was content to remain in Mason County, but not so William Bradford. That westward flowing tide planted something in him which was not to be denied when the time was ripe.

In 1824 he went to Galena, Illinois, where he worked for a time in the lead mines. Next he went to St. Louis, where he secured employment in the Berthoud & McCreery Store. In the metropolis of the West he heard things which would have caused the pulse of any young man to beat faster. General William Ashley had gone to his first rendezvous on Green River in 1823, and was off again the next year. William Becknell had led a party of men with packmules to Sante Fe in 1821 and, wonder of wonders, three covered wagons loaded with trade goods had rolled to the

Courtesy of Col. Waddell F. Smith

William Bradford Waddell. This is a photograph of an oil painting in the possession of Col. Waddell F. Smith.

same place in 1822. St. Louis business men had always wanted trade connections with the old Spanish city a thousand miles across "The Great American Desert" to the southwest. Now that they had them they dreamed great dreams and saw broad visions. Here he also heard about the lush Boon's Lick Country far up the Missouri River and also of the farthest frontier on the western boundry of the state. All of it sounded very good and, whether he knew it or not, a desire to go on west became deeply imbedded in his heart.

But the West was not to claim him yet. For some reason he returned to Kentucky and got a job clerking in a store in Washington. This did not last long. Next his father put him upon a farm. This proved to be a fortunate circumstance, for nearby lived charming, young Susan Byram. They were married January 1, 1829. With typical generosity the bride's father gave them negroes, horses, sheep, a big, fat feather-bed, and $1,500 in cash.

But farming was not the answer to the young man's desires. After some years he moved to Mayslick, Kentucky, where he opened a dry goods store. The business prospered, but Waddell was not contented. Memories of what he had heard in St. Louis, plus news of the far western border that trickled back, troubled him. At length he had to go. Selling his store and whatever else he possessed in 1835 or 1836, he took passage on an Ohio River steamboat, changed to another at St. Louis, and landed at Lexington, Missouri.

Apparently he knew what he was going to do before he left Kentucky. He built a store on the waterfront near Jack's Ferry, stocked it with goods, some of which were bought at wholesale from J. & R. Aull, and settled down to make a home for his family. He joined the Baptist Church, of which William H. Russell was a member, and devoted himself to its interests and program. In 1837 he joined Russell and others in forming the Lexington First Addition Company, and built a new brick store and hemp warehouse on North (now Main Street) and Broadway.

When the gold rush of 1849 swept across the country, Lexington became one of the main outfitting points. Here, as elsewhere, all eyes were turned toward the far-off Pacific Coast. The following year Waddell and others, among them Robert B. Bradford, his half-nephew, financed a party to go to the gold fields.

In 1853 he became a partner in Smock & Waddell, wholesale and retail merchants, and buyers of hemp, produce, etc. The following year he, with Russell, helped organize the Lexington Mutual Fire & Marine Insurance Company and became one of its directors. In 1853 the firm of Waddell & Russell contracted to deliver military supplies to Fort Riley. The amount was not large but it was important in that this was Waddell's first experience with the freighting business.

The firm secured no contract in 1854. Therefore Waddell & Russell tried the experiment of loading a wagon train with goods and sending it to California under R. W. Durham, It left the Missouri River at the usual time, and arrived in the vicinity of Sacramento on September 8, having lost one man and twenty per cent of their oxen on the way.

While the Durham train was crawling across half the Continent toward California, Waddell and Russell were negotiating the formation of a new firm with Alexander Majors of Westport. This resulted in the signing of the co-partnership agreement to become effective January 1, 1855.

It provided that the firm should engage in the business of selling goods, wares, and merchandise, general trading in stock, wagons, teams and other items used in outfitting persons for crossing the plains, and in freighting for the United States government or anyone else.

The business was to be conducted in Lexington under the name of Waddell, Russell & Company, and in Jackson County under the name of Majors & Russell. On April 10, 1855, an additional clause was added authorizing the operation of a general dry goods, grocery, and outfitting store in Leavenworth, Kansas Territory, under the name of Majors, Russell & Company. The partnership was to run two years, and the firm was capitalized at $60,000, one third of which was furnished by each of the members. In the advertisements announcing the opening of the Leavenworth store, the names Majors, Russell & Company, and Russell, Majors & Waddell were used.

It has been said again and again that Waddell furnished the money for the great undertaking they had in mind. Nothing could be further from the truth. Waddell furnished his part, and that was all. Both Russell and Majors were amply able to contribute their shares, and did so. It has also been said that Majors and Russell organized the firm and took Waddell in after it was in operation. That is not true either, as the original contract attests. The simple fact is that the three of them got together on an important proposition, pooled their finances, and launched a gigantic enterprise.

The personal characteristics of the partners were admirably adapted to the job they had in hand. Russell went East to represent the firm in Washington, New York, Philadelphia, and other places. His correspondence shows that by early 1858 he was spending most of his time in New York and Washington. Of the three, his talents were best adapted to the work assigned him. He was affable, polished, and qualified in every way to deal with bankers, department heads in Washington, congressmen, and senators.

Majors was concerned chiefly with trains upon the road and was at home only during those months when they were not running. Each season he rode horseback from one end of the route to the other. He had trains of his own in operation, a store in Denver, another in Fort Leavenworth, and a sutler's establishment at Fort Wise. His job was to see that the firm's trains got through on time, and they usually did.

Waddell's responsibility was to see that local financial affairs ran smoothly. Through its office in Lexington, managed by his son John W., he bought and sold thousands of head of cattle. He also supervised the firm's office in Leavenworth, commuting between the two towns on Missouri River steamboats.

Relations between the partners were generally harmonious, but at times Waddell became impatient with William H. Russell and other members of the organization. Sometimes he ignored requests for instructions, neglected important details, for which his son John W. took him to task, and made it difficult for his associates. Being overburdened with the details of the vast business he came to the conclusion that Russell spent too much time in New York and the East and bluntly told him to come home. At times he questioned Russell's judgement and expenditures, which was something Russell could never tolerate.

Both Majors and Waddell leaned decidedly toward the conservative side of things. Russell was exactly the opposite. He was quick to make decisions, bold in carrying them out, and implicitly believed that every enterprise with which he was connected would turn out to be a bonanza. Majors and Waddell were deliberate, conservative, slow to make decisions, and unwilling to take long chances.

The formation of this firm and its subsequent activities had a profound influence upon the economic life of both Upper Missouri and Kansas Territory. The demand for oxen, of which it owned as high as 50,000, was a boon to farmers; merchants' sales increased, volume of business for banks multiplied, while its 1700 to 2000 employees profited by steady employment. It is said that the demand for oxen laid the foundation for the great livestock business of Kansas City.

2

BACKGROUND

IN ORDER to fully understand the background and significance of the Pony Express, a brief review of some of the phases of the history of United States mail business in the decade preceding its inauguration is necessary.

The acquisition of California by the United States in 1848 made it inevitable that Americans in large numbers would emigrate there and establish homes. That was the way it always had been with new lands since the first settlers along the Atlantic seaboard moved inland. They boldly crossed the Alleghenies, claimed Kentucky, Indiana, Ohio, and Tennessee, crossed the Mississippi River, and moved onward toward the setting sun. After a brief pause along the Western Missouri border they hurdled the Great Plains and scaled the Rocky Mountains to possess Oregon.

The discovery of gold at Sutter's mill in California, January 24, 1848, merely speeded up what would have eventually happened in a more leisurely, orderly manner. In due time Americans would have gone there without the incentive of the discovery of gold. In fact they were already beginning to do so. Although common sense, backed by long experience, would indicate that haste was not the best way to populate a new country, it did not happen that way. During 1849 more than 100,000 people stampeded wildly by sea and land into California. By the middle of 1852 the population had risen to 225,000, and in 1860 it numbered 380,000.

The almost sudden appearance of huge throngs of people in a virgin, isolated region naturally created a multitude of acute problems. One of these was that of communication with the rest of the world. Having been accustomed to regular, efficient postal service at home, they immediately clamored for the same advantages in California.

Fortunately there were already arrangements of a sort for carrying the mail to Oregon. In March, 1847, a bill was passed in

Congress for the building of five steamships under the direction of the Secretary of the Navy. That official was also instructed to contract for the transportation of mail from the Atlantic Coast and New Orleans to Panama and from that point to some port in Oregon.

A contract to run ten years, from October 1, 1848, was let to A. G. Sloo of Ohio for service on the Pacific and to Arnold Harris of Arkansas for the same period of time on the Atlantic. Early in September, 1848, Sloo transferred his contract to George Law and in October Harris turned his over to William H. Aspinwall. Compensation for the entire service was fixed at $199,000 per year for once a month service.

In April, 1848, Aspinwall formed the Pacific Mail Steamship Company, which assumed responsibility for the service in the fall. At this time, and since March 1844, mail was being transported across the Isthmus of Panama by the New Granada Government for twelve cents a pound.

One of the steamers under construction, and the first to be completed, was the *California*. On October 6, 1848, she sailed from New York, bound for the West Coast by way of Cape Horn. Upon arriving at Callao, Peru, December 29, she encountered the first gold seekers who wished to go to California. She arrived on the West Coast of Panama on January 30, 1849, where four hundred people swarmed aboard to occupy quarters provided for only one hundred. Sailing on to San Francisco she arrived there February 28, 1849, thus achieving the honor of transporting the first '49ers. There her crew deserted and stampeded off to the gold fields, which delayed her return to Panama for some weeks.

The other two steamers constructed under the supervision of the Secretary of the Navy, christened *Panama* and *Oregon*, were completed early in 1849. The former set sail for California via New Orleans, Panama, and Cape Horn on March 13. At New Orleans Mrs. John Charles Fremont came aboard en route to the Pacific Coast by way of Panama. She went ashore there and crossed the Isthmus to Panama City, where she expected to take the *California* when it came down the coast on its first return voyage. The desertion of the ship's crew caused Mrs. Fremont to remain there about two months. At the end of that time her skipper succeeded in getting another crew together and returned to Panama.

About the time the *California* came in, the *Panama* also arrived. Hearing Mrs. Fremont was marooned, the skipper of the *Panama* made room for her on his already overcrowded ship. About the same time a pouch of mail arrived from the East Coast in which was a letter six months old from her husband, informing her of the disaster to his 4th exploring expedition in the rugged San Juan Mountains in what is now Southern Colorado.

The gold rush and hordes of people who took the sea route to California led Aspinwall and the Pacific Mail Company to launch a new project, the building of a fifty mile railroad across the Isthmus of Panama. In 1848 Aspinwall, Henry Chauncey, and John L. Stephens made a contract with the New Granada government for a right of way and other concessions. The line was surveyed from Navy Bay, later named Aspinwall, on the Atlantic side to Panama City on the Pacific.

The story of its construction is a saga of engineering triumph over well-nigh impossible conditions. Thousands of Americans, Central Americans, and Chinese performed herculean labors in forcing the line through steaming tropical jungles. At midnight on January 25, 1855, the last rail was laid in a torrent of rain. Next day a train passed from ocean to ocean.

From the very beginning, the people on the West Coast were dissatisfied with mail service by sea. Even the prospect of a railroad across the Isthmus of Panama failed to appease them. Many of them had come overland from the East in wagons, and they argued that mail could and indeed should be transported over the same route. Thus began a national controversy which never was settled upon its own merits. Not until steel rails spanned the Continent in 1869 did it end.

After all, the knottiest problem confronting the people of California, and the more or less lethargic Post Office Department in far-off Washington, was not how to transport mail to the Pacific Coast, but how to get it inland when it arrived. In August 1848, post offices were authorized at a number of towns including San Francisco, San Diego, and Monterey. This was a boon to the people who lived in or near those places, but it did not help the miners in the interior to any great extent.

The problem was partially solved by men like Alexander H. Todd who started a one man express service in 1849. For one dollar he registered the names of miners, and as their authorized agent called for their mail in San Francisco, Stockton, or Sacramento. His fee for delivery was an ounce of gold dust, about $4.00 for a letter, and double that amount for a newspaper. After he got started, he also carried dust from the diggings to the banks for which he charged 5% of its value. On one trip he lugged $250,000 to town in a butter keg.

The first express company of any importance to spring up was Weld & Company, which was organized in 1849. About a year later the *Alta California* remarked editorially that so many of these were starting daily that it could scarcely "keep the run of them." Adams & Company was established in 1850, and in 1852 Wells, Fargo & Company entered the California field. Such companies, with lines running north, east, and south, mostly from the San Francisco region, served the mining camps and towns very well.

In 1851 the advocates of an overland mail had their way. A contract for carrying the mail over the well-worn California trail along the Humboldt River from Sacramento to Salt Lake City once a month in thirty days was awarded to George Chorpenning. On the eastern end of the long road Samuel H. Woodson, of Independence, Missouri, had been carrying the mail between the latter city and Independence for about a year.

Chorpenning left Sacramento May 1, 1851, for his first trip with seventy or seventy-five pounds of mail upon the back of a mule. He arrived at Salt Lake City fifty-three days later, having been delayed by snow in the Sierra Nevadas. He halted in Carson Valley long enough to stake off a quarter section of land for a mail station. The town of Genoa later grew up on this site.

In the latter part of 1858 he signed a contract to carry the mail in stage coaches. A new route south of the Humboldt

River was laid out and stations established at Rush Valley, Deep Creek, Ruby Valley, and possibly Smith's Creek and Buckland's. This was on what was known as "Egan's Route," over which the Pony Express later ran. The "heavy mail," printed matter, was carried on pack mules by seven riders.

One of the factors which helped to keep the overland mail issue alive and endowed it with considerable political significance was the older controversy over the possible route of the much talked about Pacific Railroad. In January, 1853, Senator William M. Gwin of California introduced a bill which provided that a road be built from San Francisco to Albuquerque and along the Red River. It failed, but the interest awakened by the debates caused an amendment to be attached to the Army Appropriation Bill which provided that the Secretary of War should survey such routes as he thought best.

Five were surveyed and mapped, but everyone knew that only two, the Central and Southern, would receive serious consideration. Since the California Trail, overland mail, and the Pony Express followed the Central Route we confine our interest herein mostly to it.

After a number of unsuccessful attempts to pass bills authorizing an overland mail on that route, the Post Office Appropriation Bill for 1856 was amended to provide an annual payment of $300,000 for a semi-monthly service, $450,000 for a weekly service, and $600,000 for a semi-weekly service. The route was designated as No. 12,578, but neither the Central nor Southern was specified in it.

The bill also provided that the service was to be performed in four-horse coaches or spring wagons capable of carrying six passengers, three sacks of letters, and one of newspapers. The successful bidder was John Butterfield, president of the Butterfield Overland Mail Company, one of the founders of the American Express Company, and one of the greatest figures in Western transportation history. His company was created by the four great express companies, Adams, American, National, and Wells Fargo for the purpose of competing with the steamship lines. His associates were William B. Dinsmore, William G.

Fargo, James V. P. Gardner, Marcus L. Kinyon, Alexander Holland, and Hamilton Spencer.

Since no route was specified in the bill, the Postmaster General chose the Southern. Beginning at St. Louis it ran across Missouri to Little Rock, Arkansas, where it joined a line from Memphis, Tennessee. From there it ran via Preston and El Paso, Texas, to Yuma, Arizona. At that point it forked, with one branch going to San Diego and another to San Francisco. The line from the latter city to St. Louis was 2,700 miles long. When put into operation it had 800 employes, 100 Concord coaches, 1,000 horses and, mules, and many stations along the way.

Sectionalism, which had its poisonous roots in the slavery issue, was involved in this and all other matters pertaining to the overland mail, Pony Express, and railroad to the Pacific coast. Southern politicians, always intent upon the expansion of slave territory, espoused the Southern Route. Those from the North, unyielding in their opposition to that expansion, supported the Central Route.

The people of the North and West who favored the Central Route raised a storm of protest and called Butterfield's line the "Ox-bow Route," but that did no good. The first trip over it, with coaches starting simultaneously from St. Louis and San Francisco on September 15, 1858, proved that the route was feasible. On October 9 the east-bound one arrived in St. Louis, having been upon the road 23 days and 4 hours, one day and 20 hours ahead of contract time of 25 days. The westbound one reached Los Angeles on October 7, a day ahead of time and San Francisco on the 10th.

The line was a success in every way, providing one forgot its length. From twenty-one to twenty-three days was the average over it. However, even at best, it was a grueling trip. After making it, one traveler remarked that he had been "as close to hell as he ever wished to be." Meals were eaten at irregular hours, the coaches were cramped for room, there were few opportunities to wash or make a toilet, and Apaches, Comanches, and Kiowas were a constant menace. Nevertheless, it continued to operate successfully until the outbreak of the Civil War.

Meanwhile gold was discovered in Colorado, or Western Kansas, as it was then known. Another rush similar to that of 1849, only on a smaller scale, got under way immediately. The new town of Denver was laid out the same year and miners flocked into the mountains. Other towns were quickly founded and a host of people were expected to head that way in 1859.

History, so far as mail facilities were concerned, repeated itself in the new diggings. The first-comers to the new gold strike on Cherry Creek, finding themselves cut off from homefolks and friends, immediately demanded some means of communication. The nearest post office was Fort Laramie, two hundred miles to the north. The demand for mail service was so great that in the latter part of November 1858, Jim Saunders, an Indian trader, made up a list of those expecting mail and loading a small, four-horse wagon with outgoing mail, set out for the Fort with his squaw for company. He returned on January 8, 1859. His fee was fifty cents for letters and twenty-five cents for newspapers. Expressmen continued to make the trip until the early summer of 1859 when a better plan went into effect.

That plan was the organization of a stage and express line by William H. Russell and John S. Jones. Russell was a member of the giant freighting firm of Russell, Majors & Waddell and a stockholder in the Denver Town Company. Jones was also a freighter, and was at that time advertising that he was prepared to send fifty trains of twenty-five wagons each from Westport, Missouri, or Atchison, Kansas, to Denver that year. The company they organized was called the Leavenworth & Pike's Peak Express Company.

They laid out a new route over the military road to Fort Riley. From that place it followed the divide between the Republican and Solomon's Fork of the Kaw River, crossing the heads of Praire Dog, Sappa, and Cranmer Creeks to the Republican River near the mouth of Rock Creek. Keeping on the south side of that stream, it crossed the heads of Beaver, Bijou, and Kiowa Creeks and struck Cherry Creek twenty miles above its mouth. From there it ran on to Denver. The length of the line was 687 miles.

The line was equipped with New Concord coaches, with mules to draw them, and temporary stations were located about twenty-five miles apart. It was planned that the station keeper's families should live in them and that six men, four drivers and two stock tenders, should be on duty at each.

The first trip over the line began at Leavenworth April 18, 1859, with two coaches traveling together for mutual protection and assistance. They arrived in Denver on May 7, having been upon the road nineteen days. This time was expected to be shortened to six or seven days when the institution was functioning smoothly, and it was.

Twenty-three days before the first two coaches started, a train of twenty wagons set out from Leavenworth to build and equip stations. On April 8 another carrying one hundred persons, including the families of station keepers, also headed westward. Tents were set up on station sites, their occupants moved in, and plans for permanent structures made.

It so happened, however, that the new route was to enjoy only a brief existence. Before it had even become well marked, Russell bought the contract of J. M. Hockaday & Company to transport United States mail from the Missouri River to Salt Lake City by way of Fort Kearny, Julesburg, and Fort Laramie. The new route was abandoned and the line moved to that used by the Hockaday Company.

Although this removal added some miles to the distance between Leavenworth and Denver, it was the logical thing to do. The road now ran from Leavenworth northwest to Kennekuk where it joined the trail from Atchison and St. Joseph. From that point it followed the old military road to Fort Kearny. From there it ran along the south bank of the Platte River to its forks, then along the South Fork to Julesburg. There the Salt Lake City coaches forded the river and ascended Lodge Pole Creek.

The road to Denver continued up the South Platte to St. Vrain's Fort and on to Denver. Under Hockaday & Company the line was divided into three divisions: St. Joseph to Julesburg, under Charles W. Wiley; Julesburg to South Pass, under Joseph A. Slade; and South Pass to Salt Lake City, under James E.

Bromley, all of whom became employees of the Leavenworth & Pike's Peak Express Company.

When Russell took over the Hockaday line, John S. Jones acted as Route Superintendent. Not long afterward he was succeeded by Beverly D. Williams, and he in turn by Benjamin F. Ficklin. By this time the affairs of the company were in a bad way. Stock was disappearing regularly, the concern was running deeper into debt every day, and trouble was upon the horizon.

Courtesy of Library, State Historical Society of Colorado

Beverly D. Williams

Ficklin set himself the task of driving the horse thieves and shady characters out of the company and off the line.

Much of the actual clean-up work fell to Joseph A. Slade, about whom much will be said later. He did a thorough job of it and the company was no longer harassed by criminals. The residents of Denver applauded the express line and quickly came to depend upon it for contact with the world outside. Its stages ran with gratifying regularity; they brought and took out mail, and transported gold dust to Leavenworth. From every point of view, except one, it was a success. In spite of its splendid service it was a hopeless money loser.

When Russell took over the Hockaday line he secured what he had wanted for a long time, a contract to carry mail over the Central Route. Although that line covered only the eastern half as far as Salt Lake City, he no doubt felt he had taken a long step in the right direction. Complaints about the Butterfield line increased day by day and it seemed that another six year contract over the Southern Route was doubtful. Anyway, so Russell thought, he was in a position to compete with it when the time came.

When the Leavenworth & Pike's Peak Company was organized, Russell invited Majors and Waddell to become partners in it. This they declined to do. Moreover they felt the diggings in the Rocky Mountains had not as yet proved their worth and urged him to wait a while. Disregarding their advice and wishes, Russell and Jones barged ahead anyway and put the line into operation. Waddell resented their stiff-necked determination and from that day manifested a mounting spirit of criticism of Russell and his actions. Majors felt much the same way but appears to have been inclined to let Waddell speak for both of them.

Russell and Jones went heavily into debt to put the line into operation, and in spite of everything they could do, the situation grew progressively worse. Notes they had given fell due and they had no money to pay them. Bankruptcy stared them in the face. By mid-October, 1859, the concern owed $525,532. There was now only one remaining hope, that of tossing the unpalatable mess into the laps of his partners whose advice and wishes he had stubbornly flouted.

On October 28, 1859, Russell, Majors & Waddell took over the bankrupt company under a contract which provided for the organization of a new concern to transport freight and carry the United States mail. This they did, not because they wanted to, but to protect their own interests and credit. Had the Leavenworth &

Courtesy of Confederate Museum, Richmond, Virginia

Major B. F. Ficklin

John S. Jones, of Jones & Russell, Cartright & Jones, etc.

John W. Russell

Pike's Peak Express Company gone to the wall, Russell, Majors and Waddell would have been badly shaken at best.

Not long after this was done Russell returned to New York where he prepared a charter for the new concern, which was granted by the Kansas Territorial Legislature. The name he gave it was the Central Overland California & Pike's Peak Express Company. The incorporators were William H. Russell, John S. Jones, Benjamin C. Ficklin, Alexander Majors, Benjamin C. Card, Webster M. Samuel, Jerome B. Simpson, Joseph Monheimer and William B. Waddell. It was organized November 23, 1859, with Russell as president, Jerome B. Simpson as vice-president, and John W. Russell, the president's son, as secretary.

Offices were opened in St. Joseph and St. Louis, Missouri, Chicago, New York, and Washington. The capital stock was $500,000, divided into shares of $100 par value each. The actual stockholders and number of shares they held were: William H. Russell, 30; William B. Waddell, two; Alexander Majors, two; John S. Jones, four; and John W. Russell, two. Benjamin C. Ficklin was named Route Superintendent, with managerial charge of the entire line between St. Joseph and Sacramento. Much, perhaps too much authority, as shown by later developments, was delegated to him. Being a man of wide experience and extremely vigorous in action, he spared neither himself nor anyone else in getting the new company into operation.

There is no question but that one of the main purposes in forming this new company was to create an organization capable of competing with the Butterfield Overland Mail Company for the great overland mail contract. The first step, Russell felt, was a practical demonstration of the superiority of the Central Route and a conclusive refutation of the hoary argument that mail could not be carried over it the year round. These required something sensational, something that would be talked about the world over, something that would wean Congress and the Post Office Department away from the Southern Route.

In all his business career Russell had been extremely sensitive to opportunity, rapid in his appraisals of a situation, fearless where taking risks were concerned, and possessing a flawless confidence

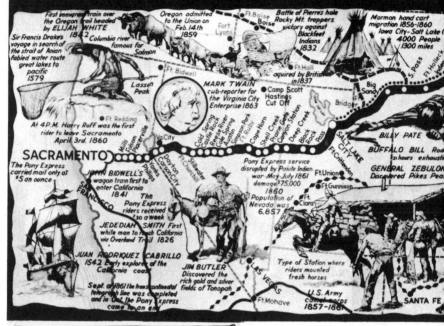

Left extremity of wall map.

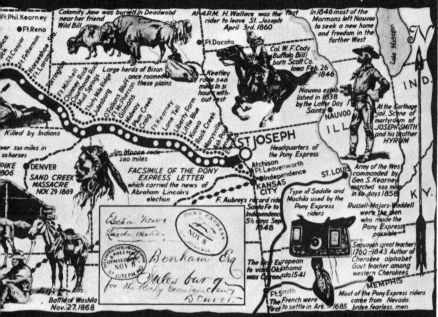

Courtesy of Harold's Club, Reno, Nevada

Twenty foot Pony Express Map painted by F. (Mike) Trevors on the walls of Harold's Club, Reno, Nevada.

Right extremity of wall map.

★ THE PONY EXPRESS ★

1860 (APR. 3) 1861

In mid-century America, Communication between St. Joseph, on the fringe of Western settlement, and gold mining communities of California, challenged the bold and made skeptical the timid. Into this picture rode the Pony Express. In rain and in snow, in sleet and in hail over moonlit prairie down tortuous mountain path harried by lurking savage, pounding Pony feet knitted together the ragged edges of a rising Nation. From these hardy Souls, who toiled over plain and mountain, that understanding might be more generally diffused, a Nation spanning a continent was ours to inherit. In the spirit of the Pony Express it is for us to bequeath to those who shall follow, new trails in the sky uniting a people in Thought and in Deed.

in his own judgment. In a letter to Waddell in mid-summer, 1860, he made an enlightening remark. "I was compelled," he said, in regard to the Central Overland California & Pike's Peak Express Company, "to build a world-wide reputation, even at considerable expense (which all things considered is quite inconsiderate) and also to incur large expenses in many ways, the details of which I cannot commit to paper."

The organization with which he meant to "build a world wide reputation" was a system of relays of swift horsemen extending from the Missouri River over the Central Route to Sacramento, California. These would ride as light as possible, carry only letters, telegrams, and newspapers, and move day and night. In other words, a Pony Express.

Here a strange thing appears. Neither Waddell nor Majors wanted the Pony Express, yet nothing they did in their whole careers sheds such luster upon their names. Majors said they agreed to it because Russell had given his word to Senator Gwin. Even so, they were not happy about it. They went along, but apparently dragged their feet.

The idea of postmen on horseback was not new. In fact they had been used in Europe and the Orient since time immemorial. They had also been employed in America from a very early date. The idea was not even new in the West or in California. As early as December 1853, copies of an important Presidential message, which had come to San Francisco via steamer, was delivered in Portland, Oregon, by relays of fast riding horsemen. These relays were set up by Adams and Wells Fargo Express companies and an historical race was run between them. Adams Express Company won it.

In every discussion of the Pony Express, the question of who originated the idea arises. Some award the palm to Senator William M. Gwin, and others to Benjamin F. Ficklin. There is evidence that John Butterfield was seriously considering one for his Southern Route, and abandoned it when he heard Russell had announced his over the Central Route. Strange indeed is it that nobody seems inclined to credit William H. Russell himself with being the originator of it. Yet strong evidence points to the fact that he was.

In his *Personal Reminiscences*, Charles R. Morehead states that Russell conceived the idea and discussed it with Secretary of War John B. Floyd in the presence of himself and James Rupe in Washington early in 1858. When Rupe's opinion was called for, he replied that it was entirely feasible.

John Scudder of Lafayette County, Missouri, writing in the *Lexington News*, August 22, 1888, says that in the winter of 1859 he, with A. B. Miller, Russell's partner in the firm of Miller, Russell & Company, and employees of Russell, Majors & Waddell were in Salt Lake City. Spurred by newspaper accounts of the overland mail controversy they began to figure time and distance over the Central Route. This resulted in a letter to Russell in which they said they would undertake to carry the mail from Sacramento to St. Joseph, Missouri, in twelve days.

Russell replied, asking for further information. They gave it, and forwarded a rough map and full particulars of the plan, which included the building of stations and setting up relays of horsemen. They were so confident of the practicability of it all that A. B. Miller offered to make a trial run over the route himself.

The next they heard about it was an order for Miller to buy 200 horses in Salt Lake City. Benjamin F. Ficklin, Joseph A. Slade, James E. Bromley, and J. H. Clute were instructed to assist him. Scudder also worked with them and helped distribute horses along the line from Salt Lake City to Platte Bridge.

From this it is evident that many minds had been busy with the idea of a Pony Express, which was only natural. Almost anyone familiar with the whole situation could have come up with it. One monumental fact remains, however, and that is Russell was the man with sufficient imagination, daring, and financial ability to transmute the idea into reality.

When the Pony Express was started April 3, 1860, the Central Overland California & Pike's Peak Express Company had a mail contract on the Central Route extending only as far as Salt Lake City. From there George Chorpenning carried it the remainder of the way in coaches and upon mules. Although he did his best under almost overwhelming circumstances, and rendered the best service possible, the Postmaster General was dissatisfied with his service. Consequently on May 11, 1860, he annulled the contract and gave it to the Central Overland California & Pike's Peak Express Company.

Russell now had contracts for carrying the mail from the Missouri River to Sacramento with pay amounting to $260,000 per year. Moreover, with a regular stage line running to Denver there was a reasonable hope of securing a contract to transport the mail to that city. With these to rely upon he felt highly optimistic about the future.

3

ORGANIZATION

ON JANUARY 27, 1860, John W. Russell, Secretary of the new Central Overland California & Pike's Peak Express Company received an historic telegram from his father, William H. Russell. It read:

"Have determined to establish a Pony Express to Sacramento, California, commencing 3rd of April. Time ten days."

John W. may have been a bit annoyed when he read it, for one of his father's characteristics was economy of words. Even in his letters he never said more than he had to, and often not as much as he should. He could, and did again and again, report or propose the spending of hundreds of thousands of dollars in less than a dozen words.

Or, what is most likely, he had received instructions from his father when he was in Leavenworth some six weeks previously. At any rate, John W. knew what was expected of him and proceeded to do it. He released the telegram to the newspapers and on January 30 the Leavenworth *Daily Times* headlined the momentous undertaking in bold type.

GREAT EXPRESS ADVENTURE
FROM LEAVENWORTH TO SACRAMENTO IN
TEN DAYS. CLEAR THE TRACK AND LET
THE PONY COME THROUGH.

Two days before this a news release in Washington stated that the government was arranging for "a horse express" from St. Joseph, Missouri, to Placerville, California, to connect with the telegraph from San Francisco, thus securing dispatches from the Pacific in ten days. This bit of news was in error, for the government had nothing to do with it. It was entirely a private enterprise.

On the day Russell sent his telegram, the Washington *Evening*

Star published an article in which it said that Benjamin C. Ficklin had left for the "Far West" to establish "an independent horse express" with the implication that the eastern terminus would be St. Joseph, Missouri. This was probably because there was telegraphic connection between New York and that place.

In the beginning Leavenworth citizens and newspapers naturally expected that their town would be chosen as headquarters for the new Central Overland California & Pike's Peak Express Company. It had been the home of the gigantic freighting firm of Russell, Majors & Waddell since 1855 and under its influence the sleepy little Missouri River town had been transformed into the roaring, bustling metropolis of the Plains.

In the fall of 1856 the partners bought some ten thousand acres of nearby land. Russell helped organize the town companies of Tecumseh, Louisana, and Rochester; the Leavenworth Fire & Marine Insurance Company; the Leavenworth, Pawnee & Western Railroad, and was a partner of Luther R. Smoot, of Washington, D. C., in the banking firm of Smoot, Russell & Company. He built an elegant home there and was regarded as the first citizen of the town.

Majors helped organize the town of Wewoka and the three invested heavily in Leavenworth real estate. Moreover, Leavenworth was the home of Jones, Russell & Company and the eastern terminus of the Leavenworth & Pike's Peak Express Company.

Although the people of Leavenworth had sufficient grounds for hope that the Central Overland California & Pike's Peak Express Company would be located there, they knew full well that St. Joseph across the river to the north was a powerful contender for the honor. Since 1854 Leavenworth had been the most influential town and one of the two most important points of entry into Kansas Territory. The Hannibal & St. Joseph Railroad had completed its line across Missouri and the telegraph came with it. That changed things materially. Therefore it was no surprise to the people of Leavenworth when on March 20, 1860, Russell and Waddell, in behalf of the Central Overland California & Pike's Peak Express Company, signed a contract with twenty representative St. Joseph citizens under which they agreed to establish headquarters there.

They also agreed to start a line of coaches from St. Joseph to Denver on a weekly schedule or more often after May 1, 1860, run a Pony Express from Wathena, Kansas to Sacramento, California as soon as the Roseport & Palmetto Railroad reached Wathena, and start a fast freight line to Denver. It was further stipulated that the Company would not be required to operate the Pony Express longer than six months if it did not pay.

On behalf of St. Joseph, the citizens agreed to give the Company twelve lots in Pattee extension; eighteen lots in the town of Elwood, Kansas just across the Missouri River near the terminus of the Roseport & Palmetto Railroad; furnish a building at Fifth and Francis; a room for an office at Second and Francis rent free for one year, and that the railroad should be in operation from St. Joseph to Wathena by May 15, 1861.

They further agreed that free passage for express matter, officers, agents, and employees of the Express company should be granted over the railroad for twelve months and ferriage across the Missouri River for coaches, wagons, etc. for two years. Perhaps the most important and intriguing clause in it provided for the exclusive privilege of carrying express over that road and its extensions and for the withholding of all connections from other railroads running west to Denver which did not grant the same.

Under the terms of this contract the way was paved for the Central Overland California & Pike's Peak Express Company to engage in a new business, the railway express business. The promoters of the Roseport & Palmetto Railroad, like those of all others, dreamed great things for their undertaking. They meant to lay their rails to Denver, and perhaps to the Pacific, if fortune favored them. Why, they asked, should not St. Joseph be the eastern terminus of the long anticipated Pacific Railroad? If it ever happened that way, Russell's company would be in a favored position indeed.

Although the Central Overland California & Pike's Peak Express Company had been incorporated and everything was now done in its name, the public, and even newspapers, for a short

time associated its activities with the defunct Leavenworth &
Pike's Peak Express Company; Jones, Russell & Company; and
Russell, Majors & Waddell. This was mostly due to the bewilder-
ing inter-locking partnerships of the four most prominent figures
in all of them, Russell, Majors, Waddell, and Jones.

Their own activities in organizing the Pony Express added to
the confusion, for on February 10, 1860, the Leavenworth *Daily
Times* carried an advertisement for "200 grey mares" over the
name of Jones, Russell & Company, the New York *Daily Tribune*
also muddied the waters by carrying an article on March 16 in
which Jones, Russell & Company was credited with launching
the enterprise.

Regardless of the fact that the Central Overland California &
Pike's Peak Express Company should be technically credited with
organizing the Pony Express it was the freighting firm of Russell,
Majors & Waddell that financed it. They satisfied the creditors
of the Leavenworth & Pike's Peak Express Company and supplied cash for establishing stations, buying supplies, horses, and
equipment, and the paying of wages to employees.

The route over which the Pony Express would run was one
of the longest overland roads in the world. Actually it measured
1966 miles from St. Joseph to Sacramento. The only one which
surpassed it in length was Butterfield's Overland Mail route far
to the south.

From St. Joseph to Fort Kearny it was mostly "prairie country" adapted to cultivation. Beyond that point, and to the Rocky
Mountains, the country was a sterile, dreary desert except for
narrow strips along streams. The mountain region extending from
South Pass to Salt Lake City was, in most places, arid, rugged,
and barren. From Salt Lake City to Carson City the route ran
through one of the worst desert regions on the North American
Continent. It was a thirsty, lonely waste, very sparsely populated
by the most degraded Indians in America.

The route was divided into five Divisions with a superintendent
appointed for each. They were as follows: St. Joseph to Fort
Kearny under A. E. Lewis whose headquarters were at St.
Joseph, Fort Kearny to Horseshoe Station above Fort Laramie

Courtesy of Utah State Historical Society

First South Street, Salt Lake City, Early 1860's. Early-day view of First South Street looking east from Main Street. The Salt Lake Theatre is shown.

under Joseph A. Slade with his home and headquarters at Horseshoe, Horseshoe Station to Salt Lake City under James E. Bromley who lived at Weber Station, Salt Lake City to Robert's Creek Station under Howard Egan whose home was in Salt Lake City and Robert's Creek to Sacramento under Bolivar Roberts who made his headquarters at Carson City.

These men were thoroughly familiar with the work they had in hand and perfectly familiar with the portion of the route under their jurisdiction. Benjamin F. Ficklin was Superintendent of the entire route and William W. Finney was Agent for the Central Overland California and Pike's Peak Express Company with an office in San Francisco. Of course it was all under the direct authority of William H. Russell who spent most of his time in the East.

Russell gave his associates and employees only sixty-five days to get ready for the great undertaking. But it was enough. Each man was given his responsibility and the whole organization moved with the precision of a military unit. Most of the actual work fell to the five Division Superintendents who took orders directly from Benjamin F. Ficklin.

Getting the line ready from St. Joseph to Julesburg was comparatively easy because some fifteen stage stations twenty-five or thirty miles apart which could be used by the Pony Express had been built by the Leavenworth & Pike's Peak Express Company about a year before. A like number of new stations to be used only by Pony Express riders for relays were quickly erected about half way between the old ones.

How many stage stations, if any, there were between Julesburg and Salt Lake City is not known. The Leavenworth & Pike's Peak Express Company got none when they bought the Hockaday mail contract in 1859. They may have built some, but if they did the number is not known. John A. Slade made the preparations from Fort Kearny to Horseshoe Station above Fort Laramie. He built stations, distributed stock, assigned riders to their posts, and appointed stationkeepers and stock tenders.

The Division from Horseshoe Station to Salt Lake City, a difficult one, was organized and put into operation by J. C. Bromley. When mail service to Salt Lake City was resumed after the "Mormon War" he was given the responsibility of reopening the line from Atchison, Kansas, to Salt Lake City. This work having been completed, he was put in charge of the road from the latter city to Pacific Springs. With the help of A. B. Miller, John Scudder and others he bought sufficient horses to send some east to John A. Slade. He employed riders, station keepers, and stock tenders, some of whom were Mormons and others French-Canadians. When the zero hour of April 3 arrived he was ready.

The portion of the route west to Salt Lake City ran past Camp Floyd through fairly well settled country. Beyond Point Lookout Station it lay through the most difficult and dangerous region on the whole line. Critics of the undertaking confidently declared that the solitary riders would all be slain by the Gosh Utes, Pah Utes, and Shoshone Indians who inhabited it. There was reasonably grounds for this gloomy prediction, for the route cut squarely across the age-old hunting grounds of these tribesmen.

Moreover, since immigration to Oregon began in 1843 the Indians had observed the increase in traffic through their country and the decrease in game animals. Common sense told them they were doomed if that sort of thing kept on. Their resentment mounted year by year and trouble for the immigrants multiplied.

To Howard Egan, noted explorer, frontiersman, and former bodyguard for Joseph Smith in Nauvoo, Illinois, was given the task of getting ready the line from Salt Lake City to Robert's Creek Station. His knowledge of the West was inferior to none, and long experience had made him familiar with the Division under his authority. Since eight or ten old Chorpenning stage stations were already in use upon it, his job was to double the number. Bill Roberts, former wagon boss for Russell, Majors & Waddell, assisted him.

Out at Sacramento and Carson City, Bolivar Roberts, also a man of wide experience and western know-how, threw himself wholeheartedly into the task of getting his Division from Roberts Creek to the former city into working order. He too had the advantage of ten or a dozen old Chorpenning stage stations to begin with. He bought 129 mules, 100 horses, hired twenty-one men as express riders and packers, and bought saddles, bridles, blankets, tents, tools, and provisions for the stations. Making up a wagon train, he headed eastward establishing stations and distributing station keepers, stock tenders, and horses.

From the very beginning such difficulties and unexpected expenses for feed, provisions, transportation etc. were encountered that the amount of money alloted William W. Finney, General Agent for the Central Overland California & Pike's Peak Express Company in California, was almost exhausted. In this crisis Ben Holladay, friend of William H. Russell and associated with him in a contract to supply flour to United States troops at Camp Floyd in 1859, cashed drafts and advanced funds to complete the work. This was an important favor, for it was the first of a series of such loans which in due time compelled him to take over the Central Overland California & Pike's Peak Express Company to protect them.

About 119 stations dotted the approximately 1,966 mile long trail between St. Joseph and Sacramento. Every 75 to 100 miles was a "Home Station" where a rider could rest for a short time before starting back. Each rider covered the route between two of these stations, changing horses on the average of six to eight times going in both directions.

A schedule, as exacting as that of a railroad timetable, was set up, and each rider was under rigid orders to keep it, day and night, fair weather or foul. Allowance was made for nothing, not even attack by Indians. Their motto was, "The mail must go through," and it did except in a very few, rare cases. As published in the St. Joseph *Weekly West* the schedule for the first run was as follows:

Marysville .... 12 hours
Fort Kearny .... 34 hours
Fort Laramie .... 80 hours
Fort Bridger ....108 hours
Great Salt Lake ....124 hours
Camp Floyd ....128 hours
Carson City ....188 hours
Placerville ....226 hours
Sacramento ....234 hours
San Francisco ....240 hours

The choice of riders was one of paramount importance. In fact the success or failure of the whole enterprise depended primarily upon them. They had to be young, good horsemen, accustomed to outdoor life, able to endure severe hardship and fatigue, and fearless. The ideal age was set at twenty, but a number considerably younger are known to have been employed. Only those of good moral character, not addicted to drink, were eligible. Upon being employed, each was required to sign the famous Majors oath and was given a Bible.

All young men on the frontier were accustomed to handling and riding horses. In the West horsemanship was like learning to walk; everybody learned it young. This particular skill was emphasized in hiring Pony Express riders because the manner in which they handled their mounts upon the road was highly important. A man who did not know how to treat an expensive animal on a ten to fifteen mile run was not wanted.

On Slade's and Lewis' Divisions the most of the riders were either natives of Missouri, Kansas or Nebraska or young men who had been drawn to the frontier from the East. Some were old employees of Russell, Majors & Waddell or some othe·· freighting concern. A few had driven stage coaches and others were veterans of the Santa Fe Trail.

On Bromley's and Egan's Divisions the majority of the riders were young Mormons whose parents had settled in Utah after 1847. Since they had grown to young manhood under unbeliev- ably severe conditions, the idea of making a continuous horse- back ride of around a hundred miles did not seem extraordinary to them at all.

What was more important, especially for those who rode the Divisions west of Salt Lake City, they had lived neighbors to Indians all their lives. Brigham Young's policy for dealing with the Utahs, Gosh Utes, Pah Utes, and Shoshones, which had always been highly successful, was that of making friends with them. The fact that the young riders knew the red man, had respect for him, and did not fear him contributed largely towar keeping the line in operation when trouble developed.

The riders were paid, on the average, $50 per month, board and room. East of Fort Kearny the home stations and meals were about what they had always known at home. West of that, however, both were incredibly primitive. The room part of it was generally a rough shack of wood, stone, or adobe or a half dug-out in a hillside, with a crude bunk with buffalo robes and blankets for a bed.

According to modern standards the pay seems small for the services rendered, but when the pay of company officials is taken into account it does not appear to be out of line. Secre- tary John W. Russell received $150 per month and Superintendent Benjamin F. Ficklin probably from $250 to $300. The five

Division Superintendents received $90 per month each. Stage drivers over the same route seem to have constituted an aristocratic class by themselves with salaries ranging up to $350 per month.

Everybody knew the job would be hard on men and horseflesh, and it was. Even under the best of conditions a ten or fifteen mile run was a grueling experience for a horse and a one hundred mile non-stop ride for a man was a terrific effort. Of the eighty riders employed in the beginning, only a few lasted through the eighteen months which followed. Some couldn't take it, others became ill, and still others found more congenial ways to make a living.

Five hundred of the best horses money could buy were required to start and keep the Pony Express in operation. On the Divisions east of Fort Laramie these were mostly high grade Kentucky stock, swift as the wind. The Western Divisions used mostly mustangs, animals native to the country and noted for their toughness and speed. Although they were given the best of feed, at great expense, and received the best of care, mortality among them must have been high and replacements numerous.

Some of the horses for the Eastern Divisions were bought from Captain McKissack, Quartermaster at Fort Leavenworth, and others in the open market. Since only the best were wanted, they cost from $150 to $200 each. The price was high, but it was not too much in view of what was expected of them. They had to make an average of 12½ miles per hour on the road with no stops between relay stations. That was a large order, even for a Kentucky thoroughbred. As later events were to prove, the life of a rider and delivery of the precious mail might depend more upon the speed of the horse than upon the fighting ability of his rider. Out-riding the Indians was always considered the best means of defence against them.

Only a few of the stations stretching half way across the Continent were near settlements or human habitations. West of Fort Kearny most of them stood in dreary solitude upon the limitless prairie or in unnamed mountain canyons. Choice of location was not governed by attractive surroundings, charming views, or beautiful scenery, but by the distance a horse could travel at maximum speed without stopping. Even the availability of water was not necessarily a matter of primary consideration, for wells were dug at some stations at the cost of considerable labor and money and the life giving liquid hauled to others in barrels.

The material of which the stations were built varied according to the region through which the route ran. Near the extreme Eastern and Western ends they were built of logs or lumber. In Nevada and Western Utah they were constructed of adobe bricks, made upon the spot, or stone laid up without mortar. In Nebraska some were put up with sod, a few near Julesburg with logs or lumber, and others with adobe bricks. Of those in Wyoming some were made of logs, others of lumber, and others of handy adobe bricks. Some were mere holes in a hillside roofed over with logs, brush, and a dirt roof.

Station keepers and stock tenders were employed at all stations, with two at those used only by the Pony Express and from four to six at those also used by the stage coaches. Their job was to take care of the two or three Pony Express horses kept at all of them and of the eight to ten stage coach mules kept at the others. There was a corral built next to the station of whatever was handy, a shed for shelter, and stalls for the animals.

While the lives of station keepers and stock tenders were monotonous, they were not as lonely as one might suppose. Pony Express riders arrived once a week at first, then twice. East of Salt Lake City stage coaches bearing passengers and mail ran past their door once or twice a week, slow motion wagon trains often stopped to inquire about the road ahead, and travelers on horseback were common. In addition, the wagon trains which supplied the stations with feed for the horses and provisions for the men appeared regularly about once a month.

West of Salt Lake City, stage coaches did not run on the route for six or eight months after midsummer of 1860 but the mail was carried through to Sacramento once a week on pack mules. Pony Express stations were used by these carriers who were always welcome visitors. Travelers on horseback to and from California frequently passed by and company wagon trains loaded with supplies called at monthly intervals or oftener. After all, these men, most of whom were inured to solitude, did not fare so badly so far as human companionship was concerned.

The quality of the station keepers and stock tenders, which was fully as high as that of the riders, is seen in the fact that when Indian trouble broke in Nevada in May, 1860, they, with rare exceptions, stuck to their posts. They could have ridden off to safety, but they did nothing of the sort. Some of them fought bravely, only to be killed in the end, their stations destroyed, and their stock driven off. Others carried on as though nothing were out of the ordinary although they knew they were in danger of attack every hour of the day and night.

When orders to equip the Central Overland California & Pike's Peak Express Company line went out, R. B. Bradford & Company, of Denver, was instructed to equip the stage stations on the branch line from that city to Julesburg. Although these were not used by the Pony Express, the items sent out reveal much of how the occupants of stations and travelers upon the road lived. The partners in this firm were R. B. Bradford, William H. Russell, Alexander Majors, and William B. Waddell. The bill was charged to the firm of Russell, Majors & Waddell.

Food items included: hams, bacon, flour, pickles, tripe, syrup, salt, tea, coffee, dried fruits, and corn meal.

For housekeeping there were: brooms, tin dishes, candles, tin and wood buckets, blankets, matches, scissors, needles, thread, stoves, axes, hammers and saws.

Stable and horse equipment consisted of: brushes, currycombs, horseshoe nails, manure forks, bridles, horse liniment, rope, farrier's tools and other items.

Medicine for man and beast is represented by such sturdy items as: turpentine, castor oil, copperas, borax, and cream of tartar.

Among the miscellaneous items were: nails, antelope skins, window sashes, screws, hinges, putty, well pulleys, wagon grease, monkey wrenches, rubber blankets, tin safes, stove dampers and twine. When the final reckoning came in early 1861, Russell, Majors & Waddell owed R. B. Bradford & Company $20,000.

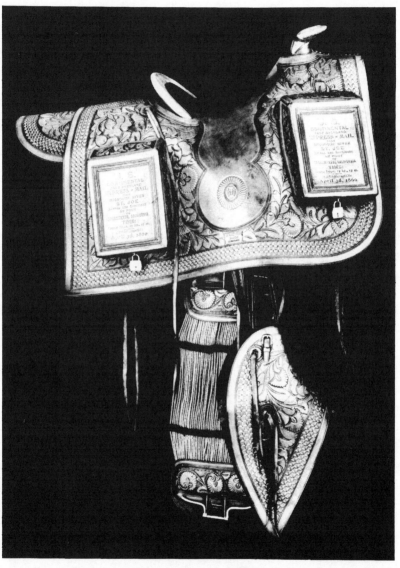

Pony Express saddle

In the very beginning the idea of using ordinary mail pouches or any modification thereof for the Pony Express was discarded. A special outer, overall covering for the skeleton, called a *mochila*, was designed. It was made of heavy leather, with a hole for the horn and a slit for the cantle. When it was in place it covered the entire saddle and reached half way to the stirrups on both sides. It was not attached anywhere and could be put on or taken off with a sweep of the arm in a matter of seconds.

Upon each of the four corners of the *mochila* a weather proof *cantina* or box of sole leather was stitched. Three of these, equipped with small padlocks, were for the "through mail" from terminus to terminus. Only the station keepers at St. Joseph and Sacramento had keys for them. The other was for mail picked up along the way and was not locked. When the *mochila* was in place, the rider sat upon it, with a leg on each side between the *cantinas*. So, as long as he remained upon his horse, there was no danger whatever of losing his precious cargo.

This simple, yet highly efficient device was a time saver in the changing of horses at relay stations. All the rider had to do was strip the *mochila* from the saddle he had been riding, fling it upon another on the back of a fresh horse, and be off again. It only required a very few seconds to do this and sometimes it was done on the run without the rider touching the ground. The system was that each *mochila* covered the entire route between St. Joseph and Sacramento, without stopping, while the saddles shuttled back and forth between relay stations.

The name of the designer of these famous saddles is not known. Perhaps they were the result of the combined ideas of a group of men, which included Israel Landis, saddle maker in St. Joseph, who manufactured many of them. It is doubtful that he was responsible for all of them, for the matter of transporting them to the West Coast would have presented a problem.

Simultaneously with the announcement of the starting of the Pony Express, advertisements under the name of the Central Overland California & Pike's Peak Express Company appeared in Washington, D. C., New York, St. Louis, Chicago, St. Joseph, Salt Lake City, Sacramento, and San Francisco newspapers. These did not reveal the Eastern terminus which was kept secret until March 31 when the St. Joseph *Weekly West* jubilantly announced that city as the chosen point. The fact that the Express would carry telegrams between the ends of the Placerville and St. Joseph telegraph wire at Carson City and St. Joseph in eight days was emphasized. Letter mail, they said, would be delivered in San Francisco ten days after departure from St. Joseph.

The route as given in these advertisements was through Forts Kearny, Laramie and Bridger, Salt Lake City, Camp Floyd, Carson City, the Washoe Silver Mines, Placerville, and Sacramento. In anticipation of a wide service, they said letters for Oregon, Washington Territory, British Columbia, the Pacific Mexican ports, Russian Possessions, Sandwich Islands, China, Japan, and India would be mailed at San Francisco to continue on their way.

Instructions for getting letters into the *cantinas* of the first rider to leave the Missouri River were explicit. In Washington, D. C. they were to be taken to 481 Tenth Street where they would be received until 2:45 p. m. on Friday, March 30th. In New York they were to be taken to the office of J. B. Simpson, vice president of the Central Overland California & Pike's Peak Express Company, No. 8 Continental Bank Building, Nassau Street, until 6:50 p. m., of March 31st. This was also William H. Russell's New York office.

The office in Chicago was located at 80 Dearborn Street, with W. H. Warder in charge, but H. J. Spaulding was agent. In St. Louis the office of Samuel & Allen, 132 North Second Street, was designated as the receiving point. The St. Joseph office was in the Pattee House, with U. Raisin in charge. Letters intended for the Pony Express could be left in all these places with the assurance they would be forwarded to St. Joseph for the historic first run.

Tradition says that the first riders out of St. Joseph wore a sort of uniform—red shirts, blue trousers, high topped boots, and broad brimmed hits. If they did it was probably more by coincidence than anything else. Red shirts, blue jeans trousers, boots, and broad brimmed hats were common with outdoor men on the frontier. So far as orders were concerned, they were probably allowed to dress as the job they had in hand demanded.

Most of those riding the Divisions west of Kansas undoubtedly wore buckskins because they were best adapted to rough life in those regions. All of them wore spurs and carried a quirt, as did horsemen everywhere. They have been pictured as wearing gauntleted white buckskin gloves, but it is doubtful that they did except when necessity demanded it.

In the beginning, those west of Fort Kearny carried a rifle, which was soon discarded, and two revolvers. One of the latter was also discarded and a loaded cylinder Colt carried in its stead. They had little need for firearms east of Julesburg, but west of Salt Lake City, as events later proved, they were a necessity. Strange to say, some kind of a little horn was carried in the beginning to warn station keepers and stock tenders of their approach. This too was quickly discarded as a nuisance. A shout from the rider and the drum of approaching hoof-beats served just as well to alert them.

Courtesy of Missouri State Historical Society

Old Patee House

Regardless of what one's opinion of Russell's soundness of judgment may be, one must accord him a high degree of administrative genius. Even the fact that in this great undertaking he enjoyed distinct advantages to begin with does not detract from what is due him. First of all there was the vast freighting firm of Russell, Majors & Waddell with its huge resources and experienced personnel. The Leavenworth & Pike's Peak Express Company was already in operation to both Denver and Salt Lake City; the resources of Miller, Russell & Company of that city were his to command, as were those of R. B. Bradford & Company of Denver.

Russell's genius is seen in the fact that he was able to harness these far-flung organizations to the speedy accomplishment of a definite task. He never doubted that the Pony Express would start on April 3, and it did. No one else doubted it either, and their faith in him was justified.

4

THEY'RE OFF!

THE ANNOUNCEMENT of the Pony Express sent a thrill through the heart of every young man along the route. Promise of good pay, adventure, congenial fellowship, and a unique job drew them like a magnet. Everyone who could do so made up his mind to get on if possible.

At St. Joseph crowds of them sought the office in Pattee House, stated their qualifications, and hoped for the best. Just who interviewed them is not known. Among the possibilities are Division Superintendent A. E. Lewis, Alexander Majors, and William H. Russell. They were all there and each probably had a hand in it.

When the job was done, about thirty riders had signed Majors' pledge, given bond for the faithful performance of their duty, and received a little Bible. They were given rooms in Pattee House, where frequent dances were held in the big ballroom. Being a unique crowd of young men, they were permitted to dance in colored shirts, blue jean pants, boots, and even spurs. It was all very gay and a most satisfactory prelude to the life of stern hardship and toil that awaited them.

Many of these young men, mostly hired for Lewis' and Slade's Divisions, lived upon farms and ranches in nearby Missouri and Kansas. Among them were John Frye, Theodore Rand, Johnson William Richardson, Gus and Charles Cliff, Henry Wallace, Jack Keetley, and Don Rising. For the most of them the idle, carefree days and nights at Pattee House were few in number. A week or so before the Pony Express started most of them were sent out along the route to the west to take their places at the lonely stations to which they had been assigned.

Among those kept in St. Joseph to ride between that place and Seneca, Kansas, the first home station to the west, were John Frye and Johnson William Richardson.

Unfortunately the identity of the first rider out of St. Joseph became an issue in a hoary controversy which will probably never be settled to everyone's satisfaction. Some ten men, all of them unquestionably riders and members of the group hired at St. Joseph, have been nominated for the honor. In recent years, however, the tendency seems to be to drop all of them except John Frye and Johnson William Richardson.

In this matter, as in many other things relating to the Pony Express, the historian is compelled to assemble all available evidence, documentary and otherwise, evaluate it to the best of his ability, and render his decision accordingly. That is what has been done here.

In 1923, Mrs. Louise Platt Hauck, of St. Joseph, a competent research worker, was asked by the committee of the St. Joseph Pony Express Celebration to make a thorough investigation of the question of the first rider. After exhaustive research she reported that an analysis of the evidence pointed clearly to Richardson. Primarily, her opinion was based upon an article in the St. Joseph *Weekly West* of April 7, 1860, which was a reprint from the April 4 daily, wherein he was specifically named. Prior to that time this copy was not known to exist.

Her search also brought to light long missing files of the St. Joseph *Missouri Free Democrat* and the Elwood, Kansas, *Free Press*. She also consulted a copy of the *Missouri Republican*. All four of the newspapers carried articles on the start of the Pony Express. One names Richardson as the first rider, another mentions a stranger, and the other two are silent on the subject. None of them mentions Frye.

In her work, Mrs. Hauck also consulted old letters, diaries, and ancient scrap-books. When her findings were completed and presented to the committee which appointed her, the committee declined to adopt them. That was understandable in view of the fact that the Frye tradition had many ardent supporters.

It seems reasonable to assume that with the account in the *Weekly West*, written within hours after the first rider took off, as a solid foundation, Mrs. Haucks' decision should be accepted.

The first letters to begin the long journey to California started from far-off Washington, D. C. on the afternoon of March 30 in a pouch carried on a train by a special messenger. Pausing in New York on the morning of the 31st to pick up letters there, he sped on westward. All went off according to plan until he arrived in Detroit, where he missed his connection by two hours. This threw him off schedule all the rest of the way.

When J. T. K. Haywood, Superintendent of the Hannibal & St. Joseph Railroad, heard what had happened, he ordered Roadmaster George H. Davis at Hannibal to make up a special train consisting of an engine and one car and hold it at Hannibal under steam and ready to go the moment the special messenger arrived. He also ordered the road cleared of other trains and all switches locked.

Davis carried out his orders, called Engineer Addison Clark, one of the best on the road, had the locomotive "Missouri" fired up, and ordered the little train placed upon the main line at the depot. Fuel agents along the line were alerted to be ready to load the tender with wood in the matter of a few seconds and a few officials were invited to make the run.

The special messenger arrived, now about two and a half hours late, Clark was told to pull the throttle all the way back and make a record that would stand for fifty years. The little train pulled out to the accompaniment of cheers from a crowd of people which had assembled to see it off. The sturdy "Missouri" responded as though she understood what was expected of her and rapidly picked up speed. Twenty, thirty, forty miles an hour she ran. The company officials clutched their seats, saw the landscape sweeping past at incredible speed, and almost wished they had not embarked upon that wild ride.

With a hiss of steam the train halted at L. S. Coleman's wood yard at Macon. He had built a platform the height of the tender upon which he placed a crowd of men with wood in their arms. The instant the train stopped they took a few steps forward, dropped their loads into the tender, and walked away. In fifteen seconds the tender was full and Clark was easing back the throttle. So it went throughout the whole run.

On April 3 flags and bunting were put on the business houses down town in St. Joseph and a holiday spirit prevailed. In the afternoon, men, women, boys, and girls crowded the streets to see the first rider take off. Everyone sensed that the event marked an epoch in the history of the town and the transportation of mail to California. To reach Sacramento in ten days was a miracle and everyone wished to see as much of its performance as possible.

Only those riders who were to make St. Joseph their head-quarters were in town now. On that momentous day they were

Courtesy of National Park Service

"First Pony Express Leaves St. Joseph" by E. Stolz.

"First Rider Leaving St. Joseph, Missouri"

not much in evidence, however, for their duties kept them close to the Pony Express stable across from Pattee Park.

The hour for the start had been set at 5:00 o'clock and as that time approached, the people drifted toward the spot where it would be made. Here the picture of what happened is blurred by conflicting statements. Some say the start was made at the United States Express office, others that it was from the post office, and still others that it was at the Pony Express stable. The St. Joseph *Gazette* the following day said that it was from the "office of the company," which was at that time in the Pattee House. Wherever it was, the crowd was there to see the rider take off.

As the hour approached, a "bright bay mare," the one chosen to make the first run, was brought to the starting point. As she was led about to warm her up, souvenir hunters plucked hairs from her tail to make rings and watch chains. Having no sympathy with that sort of cruel vandalism her keeper returned her to her stall.

When the news that the train bearing the special messenger and his pouch would be two or more hours late trickled through the crowd, a noted brass band which had been hired for the occasion did its best to entertain the people. They were first bored by the delay, then became impatient, but nobody went home. They had come to see the first rider take off and would not be denied that pleasure.

After long waiting, their patience was rewarded when the screech of the "Missouri's" whistle was heard at the edge of town. A few minutes later the little train ground to a halt at the Hannibal & St. Joseph depot. The special messenger surrendered his pouch to local company officials and his part in the colorful drama was over. Then he walked off the stage into oblivion without leaving his name and address. Since it was not necessary to take the contents of the pouch, which included special tissue paper editions of the New York *Herald* and *Tribune*, to the United States post office, they were quickly transferred to a waiting *mochila*, which also contained the letters collected at St. Joseph and a copy of the *Gazette*.

Meanwhile the bay mare had been returned to the scene. Beside her stood Richardson, eager to be off and make up as much of the lost time as possible. He, like all the other riders had become imbued with the slogan, "The mail must go through," and begrudged the time taken out for ceremonies.

Mayor M. Jeff Thompson made the first speech, in which he emphasized "the significance of the Express to our city over the Central Overland Route". A sizzling, typical frontier city political campaign, in which he was a candidate for reelection was nearing its close. With a large number of voters present, he of course could not resist the temptation to indulge in a bit of spread-eagle oratory.

Alexander Majors, assuming the role of prophet, said that the Pony Express was but the forerunner of "a more important and greater enterprise, which must soon reach its culmination, viz the construction of a road upon which a tireless iron horse will start his long overland journey, opening up as he goes, the rich meadows of nature, the fertile valleys, and crowning the eminences of the rocky range with evidences of civilization and man's irresistible mania for progression."

So far as the record goes, William H. Russell made no speech. In fact there is no record of his ever having made one anywhere in his entire career. Apparently William B. Waddell and John S. Jones were not there, but Benjamin F. Ficklin was.

When Majors concluded his speech, a cannon planted in front of Pattee House boomed a salute, The *mochila* was swung into place, Richardson stepped into the saddle, and at 7:15 started on his memorable ride with the cheers of the crowd ringing in his ears. A short ride took him to the ferry landing where a boat waited to carry him across the Missouri River to Elwood, Kansas. There another crowd cheered him on his way. One of the most thrilling undertakings in American history was now fairly launched. While Richardson pushed his way westward through the balmy spring night, the people of St. Joseph retired to their beds, happy in the thought that their's was the most promising, noted, and progressive town in the world.

There is an oft-told story that William H. Russell bet a large sum of money, the amount varying from $10,000 to $200,000 according to the ideas of the teller, that he could put the mail through from St. Joseph to Sacramento in ten days or less. Perhaps bets were made by others, but Russell certainly never made one, for the simple reason he was too near bankruptcy to risk money in that fashion. And moreover, had he done so, Majors and Waddell, being the kind of men they were, would have been mortally offended by such an act. To make it more certain that such a bet was never made, there is not the slightest evidence anywhere that Russell possessed "sporting" tendencies even in the smallest degree.

Out upon the road west of Elwood, Richardson put memories of cheering crowds out of mind and concentrated upon the task in hand. Ahead of him, all the way to Sacramento, his fellow riders were counting on him to bring that *mochila* through on schedule time. But his was a much heavier responsibility than that. He had to do his best to retrieve those lost two and a half hours. He made his first change of horses at Troy, and others at Kennekuk and Kickapoo. At 11.30 p. m. he thundered down upon the station at Granada where Don Rising impatiently waited for him. He was three quarters of an hour under schedule time and had reduced the handicap of lost time to one and three quarters hours. He pulled his horse to a sliding stop, hit the ground, and stripped the *mochila* off the saddle. Rising flung it upon his mount, leaped aboard, and was off down the trail. As the clatter of hoofs died away in the distance, Richardson's weary horse was led to its stall where it was given the very best of attention.

Dawn of April 4 greeted Rising as he approached Marysville. A townsman who saw him ride past about 8:15 said he was mounted upon a fine grey horse which was making 10 or 15 miles per hour. In thirteen hours the *mochila* was 140 miles on its way.

At Marysville, Jack Keetley settled himself in the saddle for the run to Big Sandy, the next home station. He changed horses at Hollenburg and Rock Creek, and at Big Sandy surrendered his precious charge to Henry Wallace, who raced onward with it to Liberty Farm. Thirty-four hours after leaving St. Joseph it arrived at Fort Kearny about 5:15 a. m. of the 5th. Here Barney Wintle took over and carried it to Cottonwood Spring. On the 6th, at 9:00 o'clock a. m. it passed Chimney Rock, having been on the way 61 hours and 45 minutes, during which time it had covered 535 miles.

At 6:25 p. m. on April 9 the swiftly moving *mochila* arrived in Salt Lake City after being 143 hours on the road. Since the schedule allowed only 124 hours, it was 18 hours and 45 minutes late. One can only guess how so much time was lost, but it could have been caused by storms, swollen streams, muddy road or a number of other things.

At Salt Lake City Richard Erastus "Ras" Egan took over and carried it to Rush Valley, 75 miles away, in four and a half hours. William Dennis forwarded it from Deep Creek to Egan Canyon where he turned it over to William Frederick Fisher who took it to Ruby Valley.

Out on the Pacific Coast the people of Sacramento and San Francisco eagerly awaited the historic day, April 3. After all, the Pony Express meant more to them than to anyone else in the country. They had fought a long hard battle for more rapid mail service and, while the Pony Express was not exactly what they had in mind, it encouraged them to feel that their full demands might soon be granted. What they wanted was rapid overland transportation of *all* classifications of mail, which included printed matter. The Pony Express seemed a step in the right direction.

In San Francisco the *Alta California* announced that when the hands on the clock pointed to 4.00 p. m. on April 3 a rider would take off from the door of the Alta Telegraph Company office, on Montgomery Street, with the first east bound consignment of Pony Express mail. The same newspaper urged the people of San Francisco to give the "Horse Express" a good "send-off".

The idea was adopted and those in charge of affairs got up something of a show. The *Alta California* said next day that James Randall, who was not a Pony Express rider, but dressed like one, and a little "nankeen colored pony," which was not one of the Express racers, were at the Alta Telegraph Company office at the appointed hour, ready to play their parts.

A few minutes before 4:00 o'clock the "saddle bags," probably a *mochila*, lettered "Overland Pony Express", were thrown over the saddle and the pony decoraetd with miniature flags. The bags or *mochila* contained 85 letters. Telegrams would be picked up at Carson City. A woman tied her bonnet upon the little pony's head, Randall mounted, from the wrong side, and cheered by the shouts of the people, rode down to the waterfront where the steamer *Antelope* waited to carry the mail to Sacramento.

Here, just as at St. Joseph, the picture of what happened is partially blurred in spots by lack of definite information. Did Randall ride *onto* the *Antelope*, make the trip to Sacramento, pony and all, deliver the mail to the rider there, and return to San Francisco by boat? Or did he deliver it to someone on the boat, then ride back uptown, his part in the pleasing drama finished? Apparently the latter is what he did, for the *Alta California* in its April 3 account of what was about to happen said, "Personally he (the pony) will make short work, and probably be back tonight, but by proxy he will put the west behind his heels".

Regardless of these things, the Pony Express was in operation at the western end. Whatever was done to celebrate the important event, whatever pantomime may have been staged, was wholly a secondary matter. Those 85 letters were what counted. Exactly *how* they were launched upon their long journey is vastly insignificant as compared to the fact they were actually on their way.

The fee for carrying letters in the beginning was $5.00 per half ounce. Thus the first mail out of San Francisco netted the company a minimum of $425. What additional revenue was picked up at Sacramento and at Carson City for telegrams is not known. Certain it is, however, that the combined receipts at the eastern and western ends fell far short of paying expenses. Perhaps there was something prophetic in this.

Ten hours after leaving San Francisco, at 2:00 o'clock a. m. on April 4, the *Antelope* docked at Sacramento in a rainstorm. With the exception of someone from the Express office, nobody met it. There was no reception commitee to welcome it, and no crowd on hand to bid the first rider Godspeed. Not that the good people of Sacramento were indifferent or uninformed about it. The hour of 2:00 o'clock in the morning just wasn't appropriate for a celebration.

Letters awaiting the arrival of the San Francisco mail were put into the *cantinas* along with those from that city, the *mochila* given to William ("Billy") Hamilton, and they were on their way. Ahead of him along the American Fork lay a soggy, rain-soaked road. The going was hard, it was difficult to keep the trail in the darkness, but with consummate skill he managed to reel off mile after mile.

He changed mounts at Five Mile House, Fifteen Mile House, and Mormon Tavern. At 6:45 a. m. he arrived at Placerville, having covered 45 miles in four hours, which was half an hour under schedule time. Changing horses again he was off for Sportsman's Hall, twelve miles away. He made it in an hour, and his first ride was over.

Warren Upson, son of the editor of the *Sacramento Union*, was next in line. Ahead of him lay what was, for that moment at least, the worst section of trail upon the whole route. The road was upgrade, steep in places, and rugged. The lofty Sierra Nevadas rose before him like a stupendous granite, unscalable wall. A heavy snow had fallen upon the heights and stages on the Carson City line, which had not missed a run in three years, were held up. Back in Sacramento bets were being made that he would never cross those mountains.

Here the shrewd wisdom of Division Superintendent Bolivar Roberts appears. He well knew the hazards of his division and the kind of riders he needed to overcome them. They had to be clean, courageous, experienced young men who were inured to the rigors of outdoor life under all conditions. Among the sixty applicants, he found more than enough who were qualified for the job. Warren Upson was one of the best of them.

Not long after leaving Sportman's Hall, Upson's struggle against almost overwhelming odds began. Since neither vehicle nor horseman had passed that way for several days, the sturdy little mustang was forced to break trail through the snow. At times his rider dismounted, took the lead, and opened a way for him.

Meanwhile an Arctic wind swept down upon them, driving a blanket of dry, hard snow before it. There was no danger in getting *off* the trail but the difficulty in passing *over* it seemed almost insurmountable at times. During the eighteen months the Pony Express was in operation, there were longer and more dangerous rides, several of them, but none ever surpassed this one. For sheer courage and determination in the face of natural hazards Upson's first ride stands in a class by itself.

With a feeling of exultation he reached the summit at last. The struggle had been bitter, but the worst was over. From here on the road was downhill for the remainder of the way. Late that night he rode into Carson City, having changed horses at Strawberry,

Hope Valley, Woodbridge, and Genoa and covered 85 miles. Here he rested, but the *mochila* went on.

Ahead lay the loneliest portion of the whole route. The 47 stations between Carson City and Salt Lake City were mere dots upon a desolate landscape. With one or two exceptions there were no settlements or even signs of civilization along the way. There were also Indians, but for the moment no one thought much about them.

Mile after mile and station after station was left behind as the *mochila* sped eastward. It reached Ruby Valley on April 6 and was carried on to Egan Canyon by William Frederick Fisher. From there William Dennis raced on to Deep Creek with it. Howard Egan received it at Camp Floyd, galloped into Salt Lake City, dismounted at the door of the Pony Express office on State Street at 7:45 p. m., April 7, and gave it to the next rider who dashed on eastward with it. It was now 103 hours and 45 minutes out of Sacramento.

The *Deseret News* said it arrived "inside prospectus time," which, according to the schedule published in the St. Joseph *Weekly West* allowed west bound riders 110 hours from Salt Lake City to Sacramento. Granting that those east bound had the same schedule, which they undoubtedly did, the *mochila* arrived in that city 6 hours and 15 minutes ahead of time.

In commenting upon the progress of the *mochila* eastward from that point, the *News* said the "roads were heavy and the weather stormy . . . in every way calculated to retard the operations of the company, and we are informed that the Express eastward was five hours in going from this place to Snyder's Mill, a distance of 25 miles."

Somewhere east of Salt Lake City the unrecorded meeting of the east and west bound riders occurred on Sunday, April 8. At that moment and at that point, wherever it was, the purpose of the promoters of the Pony Express was technically achieved and their faith in the possibility of it justified. The long trail had actually been covered by relays of swift horsemen. From that point on each would race over ground already marked by the trail-blazing pony going in the opposite direction.

Did those two young men halt for a moment to remark upon the enterprise in which they were engaged? Or did they pass each other with only a shout and the wave of a friendly hand? Upon these things history maintains a profound and annoying silence.

The farther east the riders went, the better became the road. Fort Bridger, South Pass, Independence Rock, and Platte Bridge were all left behind. Past Fort Laramie, Scott's Bluff, and on to Courthouse Rock they sped. Now the *mochila* was about two and three-quarters days from St. Joseph according to the time made by the west bound rider.

PONY EXPRESS RIDERS MEETING ON THE PLAINS.

Courtesy of John W. Clampitt

East Meets West from John W. Clampitt's "Echoes From the Rocky Mountains."

At Julesburg the only recorded near disaster occurred. The Platte River was swollen by recent rains but the intrepid rider plunged in to make the crossing anyway. The horse was swept off its feet and downstream into treacherous quicksand. Since time would be lost rescuing the animal the rider stripped off the *mochila*, waded ashore with it, commandeered another from a spectator, and dashed on. The crowd which had gathered to see him go by cheered him to an echo, then fished his horse out of the river. At Cottonwood Spring he gave the *mochila* to Barney Wintle, who in turn surrendered it to the next rider. From Liberty Farm, Henry Wallace carried it to Big Sandy where Jack Keetley took over. At Marysville, Don Rising got it and hustled it along to Granada where Johnson William Richardson impatiently waited to carry it to St. Joseph. It arrived about noon, and he was off.

At 4:30 he arrived at the Elwood Ferry. Half an hour later he rode through a cheering crowd, dismounted at the Pattee House, and carried the scarred *mochila* inside. It had made the long journey of almost 2000 miles and reached its destination on schedule time. The last hundred miles had been covered in eight hours. The date was April 13, 1860.

The celebration at the start of the first rider was disrupted by the delay of the train from Hannibal, but there was nothing to hamper the one staged that night. The local militiamen quickly donned their uniforms and paraded up and down the streets, occasionally pausing to joyfully discharge their muskets. Bonfires were lighted, fireworks were set off, and the cannon which had signaled the start ten days before, boomed its welcome to the first *mochila* from the west. Church bells were rung and the people roared three cheers and a tiger again and again. M. Jeff Thompson, now ex-Mayor by a vote of the people, delivered a short address and the crowd dispersed.

The 85 letters from San Francisco, plus any picked up on the way at Salt Lake City or elsewhere, were put into the post office to be dispatched eastward on the next train. Four days later those addressed to New York were delivered. The telegrams were taken to the telegraph office but were delayed there by trouble on the line between St. Joseph and St. Louis.

When the first west bound *mochila* left Ruby Valley it entered an historical vacuum. Practically nothing is known of what happened between that place and Carson City where Warren Upson impatiently waited to take it on to Sacramento. He had confidence

Courtesy of Archives and Western History Department, University of Wyoming Library

that his mates would bring it through on schedule time—and they did. It arrived on April 12 at 3:30 p. m. With a sense of triumph in his heart, he clapped spurs to his horse and headed back along his previous trail toward Sportsman's Hall. Word of his departure was flashed to Sacramento and San Francisco by telegraph.

Snow had stopped falling in the mountains, the weather had cleared, but the snow drifts which had caused him so much toil and trouble ten days before were still there. Fortunately pack trains with supplies for the Carson Valley mines, wagons, and even men on foot were now passing along the trail. At times this was an advantage, and again it was not. Time after time he was forced to leave the broken trail and flounder through deep snow to pass a train of wagons. At 1:00 o'clock p. m. on April 13 he reached Sportsman's Hall where he gave the *mochila* to William Hamilton for the last run to Sacramento. At Placerville, Hamilton was met by a cheering, enthusiastic crowd headed by Mayor Swan which escorted him into and out of town.

Although the people of Sacramento, as well as other Californians, were thrilled with the prospect of communication with St. Joseph in ten days by Pony Express, they seem to have given little or no thought during the waiting period to celebrating the arrival of the first mail from the east. At 10:00 o'clock on the morning of April 13 the *Sacramento Union*, probably just before going to press, made inquiry at the telegraph office concerning the progress of the Express rider. The report was that he had passed Genoa but had not yet arrived at Placerville. In passing on this information, the *Union* suggested that he be received with all honors. Nobody knew exactly when he would arrive, but everyone knew it would be late in the afternoon.

The townspeople adopted the *Union's* suggestion and got busy. Word was sent out that a welcoming committee on horseback would meet him at Sutter's Fort and escort him into town. About eighty citizens and fifteen Sacramento Hussars responded and formed a double line along the road over which Hamilton would pass. Flags were run up on all public buildings, placed on awning posts along J Street, and over the intersection of that thoroughfare with Third Street. Merchants hastily arranged appropriate window displays and put up signs, one of which read, "Hurrah for the Central Route!"

Word was also sent around that bells at fire engine houses and churches should be rung. A cannon, served by Young America Fire Company No. 6, was planted in the square at Tenth Street and anvils set up by other fire companies at Ninth and J and on Sixth Street.

As the afternoon waned, the crowd on J Street increased. Women climbed to balconies over the sidewalks, while boys and men perched upon roofs or anything else that provided elevation. Everybody was hilarious and the town had not known such excitement in many a day. At 5:25 p. m. observers saw a cloud of dust rolling up into the sky out on the Fort Sutter road.

"Here he comes!" was the electric word that ran the length of J Street.

The cannon boomed, the anvils replied, and the people roared cheer upon cheer. Nothing like it had ever been seen in that town before. When Hamilton reached Sutter's Fort, his mind concerned with nothing save the delivery of the *mochila*, he got the suprise of his life. Nobody had seen him off in the darkness and rain ten days before and he had no reason to think that anyone would be on hand to welcome him back. Imagine his astonishment when he rode between a double line of almost a hundred wildly cheering horsemen.

Upon his appearance the welcoming committee spurred off toward Sacramento. Being mounted upon fresh horses they quickly put Hamilton and his weary pony to the rear. Much to the disgust of both of them they had to "eat dust" the remainder of the way in.

A bigger surprise awaited Hamilton on J Street. Preceded by a single horseman bearing a small flag, his delighted escort swept through the crowd. The waving of handkerchiefs and hats, boom of cannon and anvils, and cheers of the people marked his progress to the Express office. The cannon fired forty rounds before it quit.

At the office the mail for Sacramento was quickly sorted out and the *mochila* given back to Hamilton. Remounting his horse he hurried down to the dock where the *Antelope* had waited beyond its usual sailing time to carry them to San Francisco where a bigger welcome awaited them. After a record run she was greeted at her destination about 12:38 on the morning of April 14 by clanging bells and flaming rockets.

The people of San Francisco, like those of Sacramento, were a bit tardy in making plans to celebrate the arrival of the first *mochila* from St. Joseph. When news came that it had reached Carson City, a preliminary meeting was called at Reporter's Union headquarters on April 13. Speeches were made and toasts were drunk to the Pony Express and citizens of St. Joseph. Mayor P. L. Solomon proposed one to "The mustang ponies of California; they have done more for civilization, with California boys

"Progress in the Transportation of Mail" by Chaplie Andres. Colonial post riders, stage coaches, river boats, Pony Express and trains have all carried the mail with progressive efficiency . . . That is why the United States has long enjoyed postal service and transportation facilities infinitely better than that of any other nation.

on their backs, than their mailed ancestors did in conquering the Montezumas."

Apparently plans for welcoming Hamilton and the *mochila* were made at this meeting and various committees appointed. The Monumental Fire Engine Company was requested to "fire a salute on the Plaza," and one of the committees was instructed to buy rockets. Fire Engine Companies No. 2, 5, and 6, and Hook and Ladder Company No. 2 were requested to turn out in uniform for a parade; a Grand Marshal and aides were appointed, and the California Band enlisted.

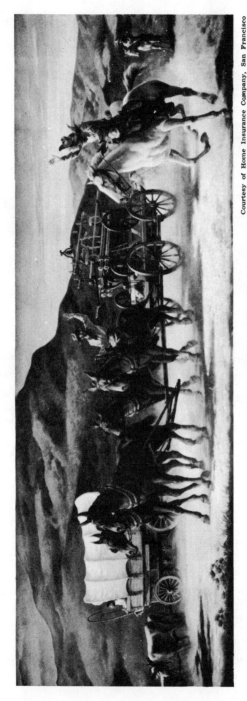

"Pony Express Rider Hailing Fire Engine Crossing the Plains" by Angelo Lanzini. The engine is a Farnham hand-drawn, end-stroke machine, the kind used in the East at the time of the Pony Express and brought to the West Coast by clipper ship or across the plains on a wagon. Well might the intrepid rider of the long trails hail this symbol of progress and protection for the fast growing towns of the West.

A large crowd assembled downtown an hour or two before the *Antelope* was due and bonfires were lighted at street intersections. The Monumental Fire Engine Company rang its bell occasionally, and Fire Engine Company No. 5 staged a run around the block to amuse the waiting people. As the *Antelope* drew in to the dock a parade was formed on the street leading to it.

When Hamilton rode his pony off the boat with the *mochila* that had left St. Joseph eleven days before, he faced his third celebration in twelve hours. The order of the parade, in which he and his pony constituted Exhibit No. 1, was as follows: California Band, Fire Engine Company No. 2, Hook and Ladder Company No. 2, Fire Engine No. 5, the Pony Express, and Citizens on Foot and Mounted.

The Grand Marshal gave the starting signal, the California Band struck up "See, The Conquering Hero Comes," the parade got into motion, and the people lining the sidewalks raised a cheer. The only hitch in the arrangements was the failure of the Monumental Fire Engine Company to fire a salute. They had received the request so late they did not have time to secure the necessary powder.

The parade stopped at the Alta Telegraph Company office, and the *mochila's* long journey from St. Joseph was over. Hearty cheers were given for the Pony Express and speeches called for. Since it was now past 1:00 o'clock in the morning and everybody was tired, those called upon tactfully declined. Another round of cheers for the Pony Express was given and everybody went home, that is everybody did except "the young fry." They stayed up the remainder of the night celebrating the historic occasion.

The Great Adventure had proved to be a practical success. Everybody knew that what had been done once could be done again—and again. That it was no longer a mere experiment was proved by the fact that the second riders from both Sacramento and St. Joseph were already on the way.

The opening round in Russell's fight to win "a world-wide reputation" had ended in dazzling victory. The Pony Express was upon everybody's tongue. Newspapers all over the land sang its praises, and in the East, front page columns of West Coast news were captioned "By Pony Express." Congressional cloak rooms in Washington buzzed with talk of it, and Russell was warmly congratulated wherever he went. He had scored heavily in his long-range campaign for the great overland mail contract, and with good luck he might achieve complete triumph in the end.

The people of California, highly delighted with the success of the enterprise, sang the praises of Russell and the Central Overland California & Pike's Peak Express Company in every possible key. They admired them all the more because the Pony Express was a strictly private undertaking of which they were the chief beneficiaries. With complete understanding that it was a bit of strategy in the old battle between the Central and Southern Routes, they threw the weight of their enthusiasm behind the former.

The remarkable success of the first riders had varying effects upon those involved in the promotion of the institution. Majors, upon whose shoulders fell most of the responsibility for the delivery of supplies to the military posts in New Mexico, gave it only minor attention.

Waddell, devoid of enthusiasm from the beginning, checked the weekly reports of receipts and disbursements and became uneasy. Public acclaim was pleasant, of course, but it took money to keep the ponies going. Where was it to come from? Consequently his letters to Russell in Washington grew more critical and acrimonious day by day. Russell replied in kind, and the breach between them widened. Nine weeks after the Pony Express was put into operation he tendered his resignation as president of the Central Overland California & Pike's Peak Express Company and offered his stock for sale.

Route Superintendent Benjamin F. Ficklin was so overjoyed with the success of it all that he planned bigger, and more expensive things. Some five weeks after the start, he appeared in Washington to urge Russell to make the service semi-weekly. Russell, fully aware of the precarious financial condition of the company promptly vetoed the idea. The result of it was a violent disagreement between them which resulted in Ficklin's dismissal a few weeks later.

5

HONOR ROLL

THE MAKING of a complete roster of riders of the Pony Express and the reconstruction of the full story of their epic deeds is impossible for a number of reasons. To begin with, no authentic list dating back to the days when it was in operation has ever been found.

When Ben Holladay took over the Central Overland California & Pike's Peak Express Company he abandoned the St. Joseph office and made Atchison, Kansas his headquarters. What became of the St. Joseph records is a matter for speculation. The same may be said for those kept in Salt Lake City, Sacramento, and San Francisco. Perhaps some of them will come to light some day, just as did the collection of papers from the personal files of William B. Waddell which the authors unearthed in Lexington, Missouri, in 1942.

The scarcity of newspapers along the Pony Express route also militated heavily against the preservation of information concerning it. The *Weekly West* and *Missouri Free Democrat* of St. Joseph, the *Free Press* of Elwood, Kansas, Salt Lake City *Deseret News*, Sacramento *Union*, and San Francisco *Alta California* constituted the list in those days. None of these, judged by modern journalistic standards, gave complete or satisfactory coverage. In many vital matters, such as chronicling the events related to it and recording the names of riders, they left much to be desired by posterity. Perhaps in all fairness it should be said that newspaper practices of the day account in part for the loss of that which everyone wishes had been treasured. In that day current events and news were subordinated to voluminous speeches by politicians, lengthy editorials, and long articles upon almost any subject, ancient or modern, except Americana. News was boiled down to the bare minimum and inserted wherever space was available.

Then too, the Pony Express, as well as many other matters, both in the East and West, was submerged by the tidal wave of Civil War which swept the country in 1860-61. News of young men riding along the Pony Express route naturally took second rank to secession, the fall of Fort Sumpter, President Lincoln's call for 75,000 volunteers, the marshaling of great armies, and the Battle of Bull Run. With events like these demanding coverage and space in the newspapers, it is understandable that matters of less interest and importance were crowded out.

To add to other difficulties, the story of the Pony Express was almost totally ignored for practically half a century. During that time the majority of those who could have told it accurately passed into the Great Beyond. By the time it was realized that here was one of the most thrilling episodes in the building of the West, much that could have been preserved was lost beyond recall.

This is particularly true where a roster of the riders and their day by day experiences on their long, lonely rides is concerned. Beginning about the first decade after the turn of the century, individuals in various parts of the country, especially in the West, began to delve into the story and write down the names of those who carried the *mochilas* from the Missouri River to the Pacific coast. They did good work against heavy odds and came up with splendid results. Today a roster bearing the names of about 120 young men, which may be considered reasonably accurate, is given below. The figures denote the number of times a name appears in the six lists consulted:

1	Alcott, Jack	6	Boulton, William
3	Avis, Henry	2	Brandenburger, John
1	Ball, L. W.	6	Brink, James W.
2	Barnell, James	2	Brown, Hugh
2	Baughn, James	6	Bucklin, James
5	Baughn, Melville	5	Burnett, John
6	Beatley, James	4	Campbell, William
4	Becker, Charles	6	Carlyle, Alex
2	Black, Thomas	6	Carr, William
4	"Boston"	5	Carrigan, William

4	Cates, William
6	Clark, James
5	Clark, Richard W.
3	Cleve, Richard
5	Cliff, Charles
5	Cliff, Gus
5	Cody, William F.
3	Cumbo, James
3	Dean, Louis
1	Dennis, William
1	Dobson, Thomas
4	Donovan, Joseph
2	Dorrington, W. E.
2	Downs, Calvin
4	Dunlap, James E.
6	Egan, Howard
1	Egan, Howard R.
3	Egan, Richard E.
6	Ellis, J. K.
6	Faust, H. J.
6	Fisher, John
3	Fisher, William Frederick
1	Flynn, Thomas
6	Frye, John
2	Gardner, George
6	Gentry, James
5	Gilson, James
3	Gilson, Samuel
1	Gleason, James
3	Gould, Frank
6	Hamilton, Samuel
1	Hamilton, William
2	Harder, George
6	Haslam, Robert
1	Helvey, Frank
3	Higginbotham, Charles
6	Hogan, Martin
4	James, William
3	Jay, David R.
5	Jenkins, William D.
3	Jobe, Samuel S.
2	Jones, William
6	Keetley, Jack

1	Kelley, Hi
6	Kelley, Jay G.
4	Kelley, Mike
4	King, Thomas O.
2	Koerner, John
2	Lawson, William
1	Little, George E.
1	Littleton, "Tough"
3	Macaulas, Sye
1	Maxfield, Elijah H.
5	McCall, J. G.
6	McDonald, James
4	McEarney, Pat
6	McNaughton, James
2	McNaughton, William
4	Martin, Robert
3	Miller, Charles B.
6	Moore, James
3	Murphy, J. H.
1	Page, William
1	Perkins, Geo. W.
4	Pridham, William
4	Ranahan, Thomas
6	Rand, Theodore ("Little Yank")
3	Randall, James
3	Reynolds, Thomas J.
2	Richardson, H.
6	Richardson, Johnson William
6	Riles, Bart
6	Rising, Don
6	Roff, Harry
3	Rush, Edward
4	Sangiovanni, G. G.
3	Seerbeck, John
2	Serish, Joseph
4	Sinclair, John
4	Streeper, William Henry
5	Spurr, George
3	Strohm, William
2	Suggett, John W.
6	Thatcher, George
1	Tuckett, Henry

2	Thompson, Charles F.	5	Westcott, Dan
2	Thompson, James M.	4	Whalen, Michael
6	Towne, George	1	"Whipsaw"
4	Tough, W. S.	2	Wilson, Elijah N.
1	Topence, Alexander	1	Wintle, Joseph B.
3	Upson, Warren	3	Worley, Henry
2	Van Blaricon, W. E.	1	Wright, Mose
6	Wallace, Henry	2	Zowgalt, Jose

In this roster there are the names of some who are known to have ridden as substitute riders, and others who only made a few runs. Though they played an humble part, they were members of that heroic band which kept the *mochilas* moving.

More or less biographical data concerning about one-third of these young centaurs of the lonely trail is available from a wide variety of sources. The others did their work, found employment elsewhere when the Pony Express was abandoned, and passed into oblivion. One reason for this is that they came from widely separated localities, and being unmarried were free to roam where fancy dictated. Some were from the East, others lived in the Middle West, still others in Utah, while those for the western end of the route were mostly from California.

Courtesy of Nebraska State Historical Society
Frank Helvey, Pony Express Rider

AVIS, HENRY was born in 1840, and while yet a boy removed from St. Louis to Kansas City with his parents. Most of the remainder of his life was spent in and around that place. While still in his middle 'teens he became an èxpert at breaking wild horses and engaged in that work around Kansas City and Fort Leavenworth.

At 18 years of age he was employed by Major Andrew Drips, fur trader, explorer, and Indian trader to accompany a train of supplies to his post near Fort Laramie. While there he was hired by J. M. Hockaday & Company, which had the contract to transport the mail from the Missouri River to Salt Lake City in four-mule wagons. His run was from Fort Laramie to that city. Presumably he became an employee of the Leavenworth & Pike's Peak Express Company when it took over the Hockaday line in 1859. How long he continued carrying the mail in wagons or stage coaches is not known, but it may have been until he became a Pony Express rider in 1861.

When he took this job he was put on Slade's division to ride between Mud Springs and Horseshoe Station west of Fort Laramie. This section lay in a region over which the Sioux Indians roamed at will. Being stirred by the white man's war far to the east, they were unusually hostile.

On one occasion he finished his ride at Horseshoe Station without difficulty but a stage driver told him a war party was reported to be lurking in the neighborhood of Deer Creek Station farther to the west. Since the rider who was to take the *mochila* refused to do so, Avis struck off with it himself. Upon arriving at Deer Creek he found that the station had been raided by the Indians and all the horses driven off. When the east bound rider declined to make his run, Avis turned back toward Horseshoe Station. He made it without being molested, having covered 220 miles. For this daring feat he received a bonus of $300. When the Pony Express was abandoned he engaged in gold mining for a few years, then returned to Kansas City where he made his permanent home. He died there March 19, 1927, at 86 years of age.

BAUGHN, MELVILLE was one of the early riders on the run be-

tween St. Joseph and Seneca, Kansas, with John Frye and Jack
Keetley. Later he was transferred farther west to ride between
Thirty-Two Mile Creek and Fort Kearny. On one occasion a
horse thief stole his pony and rode off with it. This so angered
Baughn that he set out alone to recover it. He got it, took it back
to Fort Kearny, slapped the *mochila* upon the saddle, and headed
for Thirty-two Mile Creek, where he arrived considerably behind schedule. A few years later he was hung at Seneca for
murder.

BEATLEY, JAMES, whose real name was Foote, was born in
Richmond, Virginia, about the middle 1840's. His run at one time
was from Seneca to Big Sandy, fifty miles to the west. Throughout the length of the Division he was known to have decided
preference for wild, half-broken horses. These were generally
the wiriest, toughest animals on the line. Some of them quieted
down after a few runs, but others never lost their resentment of
the saddle and bucked viciously every time it was placed upon
their backs.

BOULTON, WILLIAM was one of the oldest riders on the route,
being between thirty and forty years of age when he was hired
on Lewis' Division. Through an injury to his horse while making
a run, he was forced to strip off the *mochila* and carry it upon
his back to the next station. In later life he settled in Minnesota,
where he was still living about 1900.

CAMPBELL, WILLIAM was born in 1842 and reared in Illinois.
At 16 years of age he and an older brother went to Kansas City
where they were employed by Russell, Majors & Waddell. As
a bullwhacker he made a number of trips to Santa Fe and other
places. When it was decided to start the Pony Express he was
sent out on the route east of Salt Lake City to help build stations and supply them.

Seeing riders pass by every week, he decided he would rather
carry a *mochila* than drive a slow-motion ox-wagon. Consequently
in the summer of 1860, at 18 years of age, he was put on the
run between Valley Station and Box Elder west of Fort Kearny.

Once he was caught between home stations by a terrific blizzard which piled up snow drifts from three to six feet deep. The

trail was completely buried but he managed to keep to it by observing the tops of tall weeds in the day time and trusting the instinct of his horse at night.

When he reached Fort Kearny there was no one to carry on with the *mochilo*. Since it was contrary to the Pony Express rider's code that it should stop, he went on with it to Fairfield Station, some fifteen miles to the east, where he arrived in an exhausted condition, having been in the saddle twenty-four hours without rest. He went to bed at four o'clock in the afternoon and slept until ten o'clock the next morning.

One night he got lost along the Platte River in a thunderstorm. He heard the sound of water in the stream, but in the darkness could not tell which way it was running. Untying his lariat he cast one end into the water. It floated downstream and by this he got his bearings.

On another night he came upon a pack of wolves devouring the carcass of a buffalo. When he forced his unwilling horse past them, the fierce animals gave chase. He quickly outdistanced them and got safely away. The next day he poisoned another carcass. When he came along again he found twelve dead wolves nearby, which he skinned. He gave the hides to a Sioux squaw whom he knew and she made him a beautiful robe.

On still another night his horse, "Ragged Jim," stepped into a buffalo wallow and threw the rider over his head. Then he galloped off toward the station he had just left. Gathering up the *mochila*, which had also been thrown off, Campbell started down the trail running and shouting to attract the attention of a stage coach driver who had just passed. The driver heard him, took him aboard, and carried him to the next station where he got a horse.

The swiftest run he ever made was early in 1861 when a copy of Lincoln's first message to Congress was forwarded by Pony Express to California. Orders were sent along the line to break the record and every rider determined to do his best to comply with them. Fifteen miles an hour was announced as the schedule.

The reason for haste was that the issue of peace or war hung upon that message. People everywhere, both East and West,

Courtesy of Nebraska Library, State Historical Society

William Campbell

Courtesy of Library, State Historical Society of Colorado

William J. (Billy) Cates, Pony Express rider, carrying Lincoln's first inaugural address out of St. Joseph; he made the fastest time on record.

anxiously waited to hear what he would say. The fateful words were telegraphed to St. Joseph and delivered to the Pony Express riders. Away they raced through rain and sunshine, day and night. The *mochila* reached its destination in Sacramento in a few hours over seven days after it started from St. Joseph. The riders suffered no ill effects from their grueling experience but it cost a number of good horses their lives. Another swift ride was made to carry the news of the fall of Fort Sumter. When the Pony Express quit running, he and his brother went into the freighting business. He died at Stockton, California, in 1932 at 90 years of age, having lived to become the last surviving Pony Express rider.

CARR, WILLIAM was hanged in Carson City, Nevada, in 1860, for the murder of Bernard Cherry with whom he had quarreled some months previously at Smith's Creek Station. His was the first legal hanging in Nevada Territory, sentence having been passed by Judge John Cradlebaugh.

CARLYLE, ALEX, one of the first riders employed at St. Joseph, is credited by some with being the first rider out of that place. Being ill with tuberculosis he rode only a few months before he was compelled to retire. One day an Indian shot at him and knocked his cap from his head. After that he would never wear a cap again.

CATES, WILLIAM A. was one of the first Pony Express riders and remained with it to the end. He was a native of Illinois, having gone west at the time of the Pike's Peak gold rush. His run, from Cottonwood Springs west to Horseshoe Station, was through the sandy, windswept hills of Wyoming. He was one of the riders who bore Lincoln's first message to Congress on its history-making journey. When the ponies were dismissed he settled in Denver and engaged in business. A Pony Express celebration having been planned, he was asked to appear in the parade as a rider. No genuine saddle being available he had the local saddlemaker produce a replica of the one he had ridden many years before, *mochila* and all. He was still living in 1900.

CLIFF, CHARLES was born in St. Louis County, Missouri, in 1844, and moved to St. Joseph about 1852. In 1861 he became a Pony Express rider and was put on the run from St. Joseph to Seneca. To him riding was just plain work, since on the far eastern end of the route nothing exciting happened. When the Pony Express was discontinued he went to New Mexico where he stayed only a short time. In 1863 he hired out to an Indian trader by the name of Bowie and drove an ox-team to the neighborhood of Julesburg. The following year he went out with the same man again. On the way back from Denver, while he and a companion on horseback were rounding up the stock, the Indians unexpectedly swooped down upon them. The mounted man dashed off toward the wagon train leaving Cliff afoot and alone to do the best he could. One of them shot him in the back with an arrow. As he fell to the ground he saw the same Indian aiming another shaft at him. Springing to his feet he raced for the wagons, and made it. Seizing a revolver he faced his assailant and pulled the trigger. As he did so another arrow lodged in the lapel of his heavy army overcoat. Unable to face the barrage of bullets Cliff loosed upon him, the Indian fled. Cliff's companions removed the arrow from his back, poured raw turpentine into the wound, and put him in a wagon. Within a few weeks he was back at work again as though nothing had happened. He enlisted in the State Militia, served for a time in and around St. Joseph; then moved to a farm. Later he engaged in the feed and flour business in that city, which business he followed until retirement. He died in the City of St. Joseph December 24, 1924, at the age of 80 years.

CODY, WILLIAM FREDERICK ("Buffalo Bill") was born February 26, 1845, in Scott County, Iowa. In 1850 the family moved to LeClair, Iowa, where his father, Isaac Cody, drove stage coaches between that place and Chicago. In 1852 the elder Cody took his family to Missouri and lived in the vicinity of Weston, where he had a brother. When Kansas Territory was opened to settlement two years later he homesteaded in Salt Creek Valley some four miles northwest of Leavenworth. Here he opened a trading post. Being Free-State in sentiment he soon incurred the wrath of violent pro-slavery men. One of them stabbed him twice in a quarrel, inflicting wounds from which he never recovered.

The mother carried on, sent William to school, and permitted him to spend much time with the Kickapoo Indians on their nearby reservation, where he learned to ride and shoot. In 1857 Alexander Majors hired him to ride as messenger between wagon trains on the road to Utah. He was with wagonmaster Lewis Simpson's train on Big Sandy Creek west of South Pass the night it was captured and burned by Lot Smith, a Mormon leader.

At 15 years of age he was employed as a Pony Express rider and given a short 45 mile run from Julesburg to the west. After some months he was transferred to Slade's Division in Wyoming. With a letter of recommendation from William H. Russell in his pocket, he walked into Horseshoe Station. Slade sent him farther west to ride between Red Buttes and Three Crossings. This run, 116 miles long, was one of the most dangerous on the whole route. Upon reaching Three Crossings on one run, he found that the rider who was to take the *mochila* on west had been killed the night before. The lad changed horses and rode on. When he reached Rocky Ridge, 76 miles further on, he immediately turned back with the east bound *mochila*. He reached Red Buttes safely, having covered 384 miles, the longest Pony Express ride on record.

Numerous stories are told of young Cody's adventures as a Pony Express rider, but how many of them are true and how many pure fiction concocted by such writers as Ned Buntline will never be known. The same is true concerning his own writings in later years when his fame had become worldwide. Certain it is that in both cases imagination was allowed considerable freedom.

He enlisted in the Union Army in 1864, but never rose above the rank of private. On one occasion he was sent on a raid into Western Missouri to drive off a herd of horses the soldiers needed. One adventure of that kind was enough, for he considered that kind of warfare dishonorable. While in the army he visited St. Louis, where he met Louisa Frederici, whom he married in 1866.

After his discharge he drove horses to Fort Kearny and became a stage driver on Ben Holladay's Stage Company lines. Later, after his marriage, he returned to Salt Creek Valley, built a hotel which he called "Golden Rule House," and operated it for some time. The venture not proving successful, he closed the place and went to the neighborhood of Fort Hays, Kansas, where he and a partner by the name of Will Rose founded a town they called "Rome." This enterprise was also unsuccessful because the new Kansas Pacific Railroad started the nearby town of Hays City.

At this time the Kansas Pacific Railroad hired him to supply buffalo meat for its construction crews. Twelve animals a day was his chore. Mounting his buffalo runner, "Lucretia Borgia," and taking his .50 caliber Springfield rifle in hand, he galloped off into the prairies. Bringing down a dozen animals, whose carcasses were picked up and transported to camp in wagons, was mere play for him. It was while engaged in this work that the title "Buffalo Bill" was bestowed upon him. Near Fort Wallace he once competed with Billy Comstock, another noted plainsman, to determine which could kill the most buffalo in a given period of time. An excursion train was run from St. Louis for the occasion. Cody killed sixty-nine and Comstock forty-six.

When his work with the railroad was finished, he returned to the army as scout for General Philip Sheridan. Now he had adventures aplenty. They included one narrow escape after another. He participated in several Indian campaigns and was sent to Fort McPherson near North Platte, Nebraska, where he and his family lived in a log cabin. Here he became Justice of the Peace and closed his first marriage ceremony with the words, "Whoever God and Buffalo Bill have joined together let no man put asunder. Two dollars please."

On a trip East he met Ned Buntline, who was later to glorify him as Pony Express rider, plainsman, scout, and Indian fighter. Under Buntline's influence he went on the stage. Going to Chicago he teamed up with "Texas Jack," a former companion on the plains, in a rip-roaring blood and thunder western adventure tale which drew great crowds. While the production was at its height he was summoned to Rochester, New York, where his son, Kit Carson, was dying. After the funeral he found the stage unbearable and returned to the West.

At this time the last great conflict between Indians and white men, touched off by the Civil War, was roaring to a climax. The Custer Massacre occurred, and army leaders organized their forces to take revenge upon the Red Men. In the Black Hills, Buffalo Bill's outfit encountered the Sioux. One of the incidents in the campaign was his celebrated, much debated duel with Yellow Hand. Some accounts say Buffalo Bill killed him with a knife after both were dismounted, and others that a comrade, seeing the scout's peril, shot the Indian. Be that as it may, Buffalo Bill took Yellow Hand's scalp and sent it to Louisa in North Platte by express.

After this service with the army, he returned to the stage. This

Courtesy of Charles R. Mabey

Courtesy of Charles R. Mabey

Thomas Dobson, born June 14, 1837, Preston, Lancashire, England, and died November 6, 1916, Centerville, Utah.

Maj. Howard Egan, Oldest Pony Express rider, born June 15, 1815, Cullemore, Kings Co., Ireland, and died March 1, 1878, Salt Lake City, Utah.

led him to conceive the idea of an open air show similar to a circus. In promoting it he brought together an aggregation of genuine Indians, stagecoaches, cowboys, and buffalo which he called a "Wild West Show." It was an instantaneous success. He traveled all over the United States and took it to Europe. Financial difficulties arose later and it was taken over by others. He then traveled with circuses until 1916, when he became ill and was taken to his sister's home in Denver, Colorado, where he died January 10, 1917. In accordance with his wishes he was buried on the top of Lookout Mountain overlooking the city where his grave, his monument, and a museum are visited by thousands of tourists annually. Near Cody, Wyoming, is a statue and another museum, and in Shoshone Canyon, up which winds the Cody Road into Yellowstone Park, in his Panaska Tepee, where he spent a part of his latter years.

DOBSON, THOMAS emigrated to Utah with his family in 1856, crossed the plains in the second handcart company under Captain Edward Martin, and walked barefoot from the Sweetwater River in Wyoming to Salt Lake City. When the Pony Express was organized he was put on the run from Ruby Valley to Deep Creek. Early in October, 1860 he and James Cumbo rode into Egan's Station where they found the bodies of 18 Indians who had been slain by Lieutenant Weld's dragoons. That fall he was transferred east to ride between Salt Lake City and Pacific Springs.

EGAN, HOWARD (Major) was born in Tullemore, King's County, Ireland June 15, 1815. About 1823 his father emigrated to America and settled in New England. As was the habit of young men in that section of the country, Egan went to sea for a number of years. In 1838 he married Miss Tamson Parshley and settled in Salem, Massachusetts. There they were won to the Mormon faith by Erastus Snow. They moved to Nauvoo, Illinois, where the husband followed the trade of rope maker, which he had learned while a sailor. He became a member of the police force and one of the personal bodyguards of Joseph Smith. Later he was made a major in the Nauvoo Legion.

When the Mormons were driven out of Illinois in 1846, he and his family went with them and lived at Winter Quarters in a log cabin. While the Mormon Battalion was on the march to Santa Fe with Colonel Sterling Price's 2nd Regiment of Missouri Mounted Volunteers in that year, he and John D. Lee were sent to bring back the pay of the men for their families and the church. They overtook the regiment at Cimarron Crossing on September 17 and accompanied it to Santa Fe. Leaving there on October 19 they arrived back at Winter Quarters November 21st.

Egan was a member of the Pioneer Party of 1847 which accompanied Brigham Young on his journey to the West in search of a home for the Mormons. The following year he took his family to Utah. In 1849-50 he was a member of a party which traveled from Salt Lake City to Southern California, and in 1855 led a party which explored the famous "Egan Trail," a part of which later became the Pony Express route, from that city to Sacramento.

During that year, and for several years afterward, he worked for the Salt Lake City firm of Livingston & Kincaid, buying cattle and driving them to California. In the latter days of Chorpenning's mail contract he was superintendent of the line from Salt Lake City to Gravelly Ford on the Humboldt River.

When the Pony Express was decided upon, he was appointed Superintendent of the Division from Salt Lake City to Robert's Creek. Loading a wagon train with supplies, and accompanied by riders, station keepers, and stock tenders whom he had hired, he struck out westward, establishing stations as he went. When all was in readiness he went down to Rush Valley to be on hand if anything happened on the first run from Sacramento. It was fortunate that he did, for when William Fisher appeared, having ridden 75 miles from Fish Springs in less than five hours, changing horses five times, Egan took over the *mochila* himself for the run into Salt Lake City.

The animal he bestrode was a fiery creature that needed no urging. It was so dark upon a portion of the trip that it was impossible to see the road and a strong wind swept out of the north, driving sleet and snow before it. When he undertook to cross Mill Creek bridge his horse lost its footing and fell into the water. In a few minutes they were out and on the road again. The run was made in good time and he arrived in Salt Lake City at 11:45 p. m. April 7.

Sometime, about the middle of the 1850's, he established a ranch at Deep Creek which served first as a stage station on the Chorpenning line and later as a Pony Express station. He also opened a store in partnership with W. H. Sherman at Ruby Valley. When the Pony Express quit running, the ranch supplied hay and grain for the Central Overland California & Pike's Peak Express Company and later for Ben Holladay. In 1862 he was appointed Deputy Clerk for the United States Third Judicial Court of Utah. He died in 1878 at the age of 63 years.

EGAN, HOWARD RANSOM, son of Howard Egan, was born at Salem, Massachusetts, April 12, 1840, and settled in Utah with his parents in 1848. He divided his time between the Pony Express and the Deep Creek ranch.

Once, when a rider at Shell Creek was too sick to undertake his ride, Howard volunteered to take his place. Heading westward just at dark toward Butte Station he made good time. About the middle of Egan Canyon he saw the gleam of a camp fire up ahead. Advancing cautiously he discovered a party of Indians.

The question now was what to do. He could turn back, swing to the north, and pass through another canyon some six or eight miles away or dash boldly through the Indian camp. He chose the latter alternative, for if the savages were out to catch a Pony Express rider there was probably another party in the other canyon also.

Having made his decision he struck spurs into the horse's flanks, let out a piercing yell, and charged straight for the camp, firing his revolver into the air as he did so. Not knowing but that a large party of white men was upon them the startled Indians scuttled off in every direction. When he reached the mouth of the canyon he took a short cut across the country and reached his destination safely. Later a friendly Indian told him there had indeed been a trap set to catch a rider. They wanted to find out what he carried that made him ride so fast.

When Ben Holladay took over the Central Overland California & Pike's Peak Express Company he was at Willow Creek working as stock tender. Not wishing to continue in that capacity he resigned, went to Ruby Valley, and took up the first farm located in that vicinity. Not long afterward he went to the Deep Creek ranch, where he remained until 1870. In that year he moved to Richmond, Utah, where he and his brother William M. operated a farm and sawmill for many years. He died in 1916.

EGAN, RICHARD ERASMUS, son of Howard Egan, was born in Salem, Massachusetts, March 29, 1842. He went with his parents to Nauvoo, Illinois, and later to Salt Lake City, where he married Miss Mary Minnie Fisher, sister of Pony Express riders William Frederick and John Fisher, in 1861. He carried the first west bound *mochila* out of Salt Lake City to Rush Valley, a distance of 75 miles in four and one-half hours.

During the winter of 1860-61 he rode the 50 miles from that city to Fort Crittenden and at sundown started on to Rush Valley in a heavy snowstorm. The snow was knee deep to his horse, it was so dark he could not see the road, and he had to depend upon the animal's instinct to stay in the trail.

Keeping the wind upon his right cheek he traveled all night, only to find himself back at Fort Crittenden when morning came. The wind had changed direction during the night so that instead of going west as he had intended, he rode in a wide circle. Changing back to the horse he had ridden from Salt Lake City he continued his run to Rush Valley without rest. When he arrived he had covered 150 miles in continuous riding.

The longest ride he ever made was the result of a scheme hatched up with one of the Fisher brothers whereby the latter could get to Salt Lake City to see his sweetheart. They met on the road at night, and instead of exchanging *mochilas* each rode ahead over the road the other had just traveled. When Egan met the next east bound rider he was 165 miles from Salt Lake City. Without time out for rest he changed horses and headed back home. When he arrived he had covered 330 miles, but was

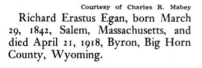

Courtesy of Charles R. Mabey
Richard Erastus Egan, born March 29, 1842, Salem, Massachusetts, and died April 21, 1918, Byron, Big Horn County, Wyoming.

satisfied with the knowledge he had ably assisted true love to run its course.

After the Pony Express ceased running, he lived at Deep Creek ranch for some time, then was sent on a mission to England by the Mormon Church. After serving as president of the Birmingham Conference he returned to Utah and operated a farm in Ruby Valley which his brother Howard had opened. Later he moved to Bountiful, Utah, where he served as Bishop for many years. Later, he moved to Byron, Wyoming, where he was still living in 1916.

FAUST, J. H. ("Doc") was station keeper and sometimes rider at Faust's Station 75 miles southwest of Salt Lake City. It was strategically located and was first called Rush Valley. It was also known as Pass Station. In later life Faust studied medicine and became an outstanding physician.

FLYNN, THOMAS rode the section between Genoa and Sink of the Carson. One day in 1861, not being met by the rider from the east, he rode on to Dry Creek. There he found six terrified emigrants barricaded in the station to stand off an Indian attack. The station keeper had been killed.

FISHER, WILLIAM FREDERICK was born at Woolwich, Kent County, England, November 6, 1839. At fifteen years of age he left that country with his parents and after a six weeks ocean voyage landed at New Orleans May 29, 1854. On the following October 28 the family reached Salt Lake City.

Fisher was among the first riders hired by Howard Egan in 1860. His first run was from Ruby Valley to Shell Creek. In July 1860 he was transferred to the section between Salt Lake City and Rush Valley. The rider with the first *mochila* from Sacramento reached Ruby Valley in the early morning hours of April 6. Fisher took it on to Egan Canyon, where he turned it over to William Dennis.

On June 17, six weeks and eleven days after he made his first ride, he wrote his sweetheart, Miss M. Van Etten of Salt Lake City, "The Indians are raising the devil out here now, but I think they will soon stop, as the troops have come to our assistance." The Indian disturbance to which he referred was the Pah Ute War.

After he was transferred to the Salt Lake City-Rush Valley run, he had an adventure which might have cost him his life. On January 22, 1861, not long after he married Miss Van Etten, he set out from Rush Valley for Salt Lake City. Before he had gone a mile a terrific snowstorm howled down upon him. When he reached Camp Floyd the blizzard was so thick he had difficulty finding the station. The men there advised him to wait until the storm was over but his reply was, "The mail must go through."

Off into the storm he rode. Some time later he almost collided with the lead team of a Russell, Majors & Waddell wagon train bound for Camp Floyd, whose boss urged him to camp with them until the weather cleared. Declining the invitation he rode on.

About an hour later he found himself lost among some cedar covered hills. After riding about for a time in an effort to get his bearings, he dismounted, turned the tail of his horse to the

Courtesy of Mrs. Minnie J. Fisher Ellsworth

John Fisher, center; William F. ("Billy") Fisher, right

wind, and sat down in the snow beside a cedar tree which partly shielded him from the storm. Soon he began to feel drowsy. Just as he was about to fall asleep a jack rabbit jumped upon his legs. This roused him enough that he realized his danger. Getting to his feet he stamped upon the snow and threshed his arms about until he was fully awake and partly warmed. Climbing upon his horse he tied the bridle reins together, took a firm grip upon the saddle horn, and gave the animal its 'head." After about an hour he found himself on the bank of the River Jordan and knew where he was. Following the stream he came to the town of Lehi whose people gave him coffee and food.

When he was warmed and rested, he mounted his horse and again headed for Salt Lake City, as he thought. At the end of a few hours he was halted by a deep ravine filled with snow. Now he realized he was lost again. Fortunately he saw a light shining from the window of a ranch house across the ravine. Dismounting he left his horse where it was and wallowed through the snow to the house. The kindly disposed inhabitants took him in and one of the men got his horse. After being fed, rested, and warmed he went on to Rockwell's Station. There he got a fresh horse which took him to Salt Lake City, where he arrived about four o'clock in the morning.

When the Pony Express stopped running, he worked for the Holladay Overland Mail Company handling horses, putting up hay, and hauling it to various stations. While engaged in this work he served as clerk in a sort of vigilante court which sentenced Ransome Young and another horse thief by the name of Webb to be hung from the rear end of a high wagon box.

In the latter 1860's he worked as foreman of a construction crew on the Central Pacific Railroad. In 1870 he moved to Bountiful, Utah, and later to Richmond, same state. Eight years later he moved to Oxford, Idaho, where he was ordained Bishop in 1879. Here he developed one of the finest ranches in the country, raised hay and grain, and bred some of the best race horses of the day.

In 1878-79 he was Secretary of the Idaho Territorial Convention. During the same period he was admitted to the bar of Idaho and that of Utah in 1883. Being a man of multiple capacities and talents, and ready to undertake anything, he bought a complete outfit of dentist's extraction instruments in 1890. During the next fifteen years he pulled about a thousand teeth.

His home was noted for its hospitality, and social gatherings in it were frequent. On such occasions he entertained his guests by playing the banjo and singing such songs as "Carry Me Back To Old Virginia," "I'll Take You Home Again Kathleen," and "Sailing, Sailing Over The Bounding Main," etc. In 1918 he sold his store, which he had operated for 40 years, and moved to Rigby, Idaho. There he died September 30, 1919.

FISHER, JOHN, brother of William Frederick Fisher, was born in Woolwich, Kent County, England, February 7, 1842. In 1860, at 18 years of age, Howard Egan put him on as Pony Express rider on the Division from Salt Lake City to Robert's Creek. He had various adventures as a Pony Express rider and when it quit running he became a stage driver between Salt Lake City and Shell Creek, Nevada, a distance of 250 miles. Later, he married and settled at Bountiful, Utah, where he became Mayor, Justice of the Peace, and member of the Utah Territorial Legislature.

6

HONOR ROLL (continued)

Frye, John ("Johnnie"), sometimes spelled "Frey," was one of the four riders on the run between St. Joseph and Seneca. He lived on a ranch in Kansas and before the days of the Pony Express was an employee of Russell, Majors & Waddell in their freighting business. Weighing only 125 pounds he frequently rode in local horse races. He was well known in St. Joseph and vicinity.

A charming story is told of how the young women would wait for him along the trail with cakes, cookies, and other culinary dainties. These he snatched from their hands on the run and ate them as he galloped along. They noticed that he had trouble with the cookies, for he could hold them with only one hand. The other was required to manage his horse. It occurred to them that if they made them with a hole in the center he could stick them upon his fingers and get along nicely. Thus was born the well known doughnut.

An equally charming one concerns the making of a "Log Cabin" quilt. Frye wore a red necktie which the young lady seamstress wished very much to sew into the article. Frye, however, liked the tie himself and would not give it up. Consequently she resorted to a bit of strategy. Next time he was due to come along, she mounted a horse and rode down the trail to meet him. When he came by she fell in beside him and again asked for the tie.

In a spirit of mischief Frye put spurs to his horse and dashed ahead. Not to be outdone she applied the quirt to her horse and soon overtook him. She made a grab for the tie, missed it, and got hold of his shirt tail. A piece of it tore off. With great glee she carried it home and sewed it into the quilt where she had planned to put the tie.

After the Pony Express was discontinued, Frye enlisted in the

Federal army as a scout. He was killed in a fight with Arkansas Rangers on the Canadian River. Captain Levi Hensel, formerly the well-known blacksmith and horseshoer at Seneca, Kansas, said he saw him within a few minutes after it happened. Tradition says that before he went down he accounted for five of the enemy.

GILSON, SAMUEL became Deputy United States Marshal when his days on the Pony Express were over. While on a prospecting trip he discovered the mineral later known as "gilsonite." Later he was connected with ranching and mines in Utah.

HAMILTON, WILLIAM was hired for Bolivar Robert's Division not only because he was an excellent horseman but because he was familiar with the country through which the route passed. He took the first *mochila* off the boat from San Francisco at Sacramento and galloped off into the darkness and ran toward

"Johnny Frye Loses His Shirt Tail," by C. M. Jsmert, drawn especially for this volume.

Sportsman's Hall. That was the end of his run. When the first west bound one arrived on April 13 he was eagerly waiting for it. He carried it through Placerville and on to Sacramento where he boarded the *Antelope*, horse and all, for San Francisco.

HASLAM, ROBERT ("Pony Bob") was one of the most daring, resourceful, and best known riders on the route. Fear and hesitancy in the face of duty were unknown to him. He was hired by Bolivar Roberts, helped build the stations, and was then put on the run from Friday's Station at the foot of Lake Tahoe to Buckland's 75 miles to the east. This appears to have been his section during the entire life of the Pony Express. During the Pah Ute War he made one of the longest, most dangerous rides on the records of the institution.

When the completion of the telegraph line from the Missouri River to Sacramento put the Pony Express out of business, Wells, Fargo & Company, agent for the Central Overland California & Pike's Peak Company on the section from San Francisco to Virginia City after early summer, 1861, continued to operate the line as its own enterprise. Haslam stayed on his old run until the building of the railroad across the Sierra Nevada mountains put him out of business. Then he was transferred to a new line, operated by Wells, Fargo & Company, between Virginia City and Reno, 23 miles away. The Pacific Union Express Company also opened a stage line and Pony Express in competition with Wells, Fargo & Company. One result of this was frequent races between Haslam and his competitors.

On July 4, 1868 he and Frank Henderson staged one of the fastest of these, beginning at Reno. They received their mail pouches simultaneously before the train came to a halt, but Henderson got off first with about a ten yard lead. Before the first mile was covered, however, Haslam had passed him and was slowly drawing ahead. To make it really a fast race each had four waiting horses ahead of him placed about four miles apart. Haslam kept his lead and won by a close margin. The driver of the Wells, Fargo & Company Lightning Express, a light buckboard, who left Reno at the same time they did and almost kept up with them, boasted that he could have beaten them both if he had had relays as they had.

When the telegraph line between Virginia City and Reno was built, Haslam was transferred to the Wells, Fargo & Company stage and Pony Express line in Montana where he rode from Queen's River to Owyhee River, a distance of 100 miles. During the Modoc War his station keeper was killed and he saw the bodies of ninety Chinese the Indians had slain strewn along the road.

About this time, for some reason, he resigned his job and went to Salt Lake City. The day after he left, Sye Macaulas, another old Pony Express rider, was killed on the route. After serving for a time as Deputy United States Marshal in that city he took the job of messenger on the Wells, Fargo & Company stage line between there and Denver. He kept this for several years, then went to Chicago to work in the Hotel Congress. He got up a personal business card with a sketch of himself as a Pony Express rider at the age of twenty and entertained guests with stories of his adventures. He died there in 1912, at the age of 72 years.

HOGAN, MARTIN, one of the first hired by Division Superintendent A. E. Lewis, stayed with the job to the end. Afterward he made his home at Atchison, Kansas.

JAMES, WILLIAM was born in Lynchburg, Virginia, in 1843. When he was five years of age he crossed the plains to Utah with his parents. In 1861 he was hired as a Pony Express rider and put on the run from Simpson's Park to Cold Springs on Bolivar Roberts' Division.

JAY, DAVID ROBERT was born at Lancaster, Missouri, January 27, 1847. In 1854, his father having been killed in an accident, he, with his mother and grandmother, joined a party of relatives and neighbors who were emigrating to Oregon. Being forbidden by army officers at Fort Riley to go on because of Indian troubles in the West, they took claim son the site of present Manhattan.

In 1860 he walked from his home to Marysville where, in spite of the fact he was not yet fourteen years of age, he was hired as a Pony Express rider. His first run was from Seneca to Big

Sandy. Later he rode from Big Sandy to Fort Kearny, with an occasional run to Julesburg.

On February 16, 1864 he enlisted in Company A, Eleventh Kansas Cavalry, and served in it throughout the remainder of the war. This regiment, originally recruited as an infantry unit, was mounted as cavalry in 1863. His company, under Captain Henry E. Palmer, fought the advance guard of General Sterling Price's army from Warrensburg, Missouri, to Westport where it participated in the battle by that name in October 1864. Immediately afterward the regiment helped drive the shattered remnants of Price's army south of the Arkansas River.

After a few months service in Arkansas and Indian Territory it was returned to Fort Riley, Kansas, late in 1864. In February 1865 it was ordered to North Platte, Nebraska, to guard the Overland Route against Indian depredations. Some of the companies participated in the Battle of Platte Bridge and about August 1, 1865 it was returned to Fort Leavenworth where it was mus-

Courtesy of Mrs. Nara M. Craig
David R. Jay, Pony Express Rider

Courtesy of Public Library, Leavenworth, Kansas
Jack H. Keetley when he was a Pony Express rider.

tered out of service the latter part of September. After receiving his discharge, Jay resumed his occupation of stone mason. On December 6, 1869 he was married to Miss Emily C. Mize at Louisville, Kansas. They made their home at Fairview, same state, until 1881 when the family moved to Atchison. He died there June 12, 1930 at 83 years of age.

KELLEY, J. G. was one of the men hired by Bolivar Roberts at Carson City in the beginning. He was therefore one of the initial party which went out with a wagon train to locate and build stations as far east as Robert's Creek. They built corduroy roads of willows in Carson Sink, fought hordes of mosquitoes while doing so, and erected a station house, which they called a fort, with adobe bricks. In preparing them they tramped the mud to proper consistency with their bare feet. This required a week or more of time and when they were through, the skin had peeled from the soles of their feet. They also built another so-called fort at Sand Springs where Kelley was assigned as assistant station keeper under James McNaughton.

When Indian troubles started in May of 1860 sentinels were posted with orders to shoot if any were seen skulking about the place. One night Kelley saw one not far away, shot at him, and missed. They saw Indian camp fires on the hills and next morning found numerous tracks about the station. Undoubtedly they had intended to drive off the horses and possibly kill the men. That day a rider, a Mexican, came in with a bullet hole through his body. He had been shot by Indians in Quaking Asp Grove and died before many hours had passed.

Since Kelley was the lightest man at the station, he was asked to take the Mexican's *mochila* on. He made the trip safely without seeing any Indians and was on the way back when he reached the grove where his comrade had been shot. A trail, two miles long, and just wide enough to allow a horse to pass, had been cut through the aspens. It was so crooked that one could sometimes see no more than ten or fifteen yards ahead.

Since it was a perfect place for an ambush, he dropped the bridle reins upon his horse's neck, took his Sharps rifle in hand,

and putting spurs to his mount, flashed safely through the grove at full speed. At the top of a hill he stopped to let his horse rest. Seeing movements among some bushes he fired into them again and again with his rifle. The movements stopped, a sure sign there were Indians among them. A few days later some soldiers passing the same spot were fired upon and killed by Indians among those same bushes.

On another occasion when he rounded a bend in the trail, the driver of an emigrant wagon took a shot at him with a rifle. When he stopped and inquired into the matter the emigrant said, "I thought you were an Indian." When the ponies quit running he became an eminent mining engineer and lived in Denver.

KELLEY, MIKE was another one of those hired by Bolivar Roberts for his Division from Sacramento to Robert's Creek.

KEETLEY, JACK was born November 28, 1841, perhaps in England. At 19 years of age he was hired by A. E. Lewis for his Division and put on the run from Marysville to Big Sandy. He was one of those who rode the Pony Express during the entire 18 months of its existence. After it was disbanded he went to Salt Lake City where he engaged in mining. His longest ride, upon which he doubled back for another rider, ended at Seneca where he was taken from the saddle sound asleep. He had ridden 340 miles in thirty-one hours without stopping to rest or eat. His wife was the former Miss Margaret Ochiltree.

For many years prior to 1902 he was superintendent of the Little Bell mine near Park City, Utah, and for four years afterward he served in the same capacity at the Silver King mine near the same place. He died at Salt Lake City October 2, 1912 at 71 years of age, and is buried there.

KING, THOMAS OWEN helped build the stations east of Salt Lake City and when the Pony Express started was put on Bromley's Division between that city and Fort Bridger. On the first run in April, 1860, he started out in good weather. By the time he had gone twenty miles, a heavy storm was upon him. The trail was narrow and slippery. The horse stumbled, King was thrown off, and the *mochila* went sailing over a cliff. After much labor he recovered it, remounted his horse, and made such good time from there on that he arrived at the end of his run on schedule.

His longest ride was from Salt Lake City to Ham's Fork, 110 miles in thirteen hours. One night he came into Bear River station and reported that he had not met Henry Worley who was riding in the opposite direction. Worley made the same report concerning King at his next stop. The truth was they had passed each other on the trail as usual, but both were sound asleep in the saddle when they did so.

LITTLE, GEORGE EDWIN was born in Nauvoo, Illinois, August 6, 1844. His family started for Salt Lake City with the first company of emigrants in 1848 but the father died on the way, leaving the mother to drive an ox-wagon the remainder of the way alone.

Although he was not yet 16 years of age when the Pony Express was started, he was hired and put on the run from Salt Lake City to Rocky Ridge on Bromley's Division.

On one ride he encountered such a heavy snow storm that his horse gave out. Cutting open the *cantinas* he removed the mail, stuffed it inside his shirt and went on to Salt Lake City afoot. The people so admired his courage and fortitude that they held an impromptu celebration in his honor.

On another occasion he was stopped by two bandits with masks over their faces. Instead of submitting to being robbed he put spurs to his horse and made his escape. Angered by this the bandits fired several shots at him, but fortunately none of them took effect. He was married to Miss Martha Taylor in 1862. On December 27, 1916 he died at Teton Basin, Idaho, at the age of 72 years.

McCALL, J. G. was not a rider for the Pony Express but he made one ride under such interesting circumstances that it is worth recalling. One day on the run between Folsom and Sacramento the regular rider was thrown from his horse and his leg was broken. A Wells Fargo stage coach, upon which McCall, special agent for the company was riding, came along. Seeing the situation he volunteered to finish the run for the injured rider. When he arrived at Sacramento, only an hour and a half behind schedule, the townspeople gave him a rousing welcome.

MAXFIELD, ELIJAH H. was born on Prince Edward Island, Canada, November 5, 1832, went to Utah in 1851, and married Helen A. Tanner the same year. He served as a spy in Johnston's Army of Utah, drove stage coaches, was a Pony Express rider, and a member of Brigham Young's XY Express Company. He spent the last years of his life in Wayne County, Utah.

MOORE, JAMES was among the first riders hired at St. Joseph for Lewis' Division. His run was between Midway and Julesburg. On June 8, 1860 his *mochila* bore government dispatches marked "urgent." He rushed it westward to Julesburg, where he arrived tired, hungry, and sleepy. He died at Cheyenne, Wyoming.

PAGE, WILLIAM was born in Birmingham, England, August 4, 1838. He and his family were members of Captain Edward Martin's handcart emigration company in the fall and winter of 1856. After his arrival in Utah he lived in Salt Lake City and Bountiful. During the Mormon troubles of 1857-58 he joined the militia under General Daniel H. Wells and was stationed in Echo Canyon. In 1860 James Bromley hired him to ride on his Division east of Salt Lake City. He joined Captain Arton's company of

Courtesy of Charles R. Mabey
William Page, born Aug. 4, 1838, Birmingham, England, and died May 28, 1893, Woods Cross, Utah.

emigrants to Arizona and died May 28, 1892, at the age of 68 years.

PERKINS, GEORGE WASHINGTON ("WASH") settled in Salt Lake City in 1848. Although not a regular Pony Express rider he was available when a substitute was needed. His first experience with mail lines was in helping establish the Chorpenning route along the Humboldt River to Salt Lake City in 1851. It was upon this line that Absalom Woodward and two of his men were killed by Indians later in that year. While on this job he saw a stagecoach whose driver and passengers had been killed and scalped by Indians. The mail bag had been cut open and letters scattered through the sagebrush. When the Pah Ute War broke out he was on the run between Simpson's Park and Ruby Valley.

RAND, THEODORE ("LITTLE YANK") was born at Plattsburg, New York February 4, 1837 and emigrated to the West in 1856. At the age of 23 years he was hired on Lewis' Division in 1860 and took the first herd of horses out of St. Joseph to stock the line. His permanent run was from Box Elder to Julesburg. One of his most outstanding characteristics was smallness of stature which, together with the fact that he hailed from New York, won him the nickname of "Little Yank." Later in life he was employed by the Missouri Pacific Railroad Company in Atchison, Kansas, where he died December 27, 1904.

RANAHAN, THOMAS J. ("HAPPY TOM") was born in Ireland November 28, 1839, and came to America with his family in 1841. They settled in Vermont not far from the ancestral home of President Calvin Coolidge. In 1855 the Ranahan family, in company with eighty others, emigrated to Kansas Territory where Thomas grew to manhood. In 1859 he became a bullwhacker in Russell, Majors & Waddel's wagon trains. After serving there for a short time, he was hired by the Leavenworth & Pike's Peak Express Company as a stage driver. From that time on his work was mainly in that capacity. When the Pony Express was started he was listed as a substitute rider on Bromley's Division from Pacific Springs to Green River.

Early in 1861 he arrived at Green River and heard rumors of

trouble. The station keeper, whose sympathies lay with the Confederacy, became angry when one of the stage drivers on the line, known as "Rowdy Pete," walked into the station wearing a small United States flag. After some heated words the station keeper ordered him to take it off and not wear it any more.

Naturally there was much talk about the incident, and since "Rowdy Pete" was due from the west any moment, Ranahan delayed his departure a few minutes to see what would happen. To the amazement of everyone, and much to the delight of Union sympathizers about the place, "Rowdy Pete" swept in, his coach, down to the wheels, decorated with United States flags. Since a big majority of those present were for the driver, the station keeper had nothing to say.

When Ben Holladay took over the Central Overland California & Pike's Peak Express Company in 1862, Ranahan continued as stage driver. Three years later, when Wells, Fargo & Company bought out Holladay, he continued working for him.

In 1868 when Lieutenant General P. H. Sheridan ordered Lieutenant Colonel George A. Forsyth to recruit fifty "first class frontiersmen" to serve as scouts against the Indians, Ranahan was one of the first to enroll. The company set out from Fort Wallace September 5th and marched to Sheridan, Kansas, where a wagon train had been attacked and two teamsters killed.

From that place they trailed the maurauders northward. On the morning of the 17th they were attacked by a combined force of Cheyennes, Ogallalla and Brule Sioux, and Dog soldiers numbering almost a thousand under command of famous Roman Nose.

The Scouts took refuge upon a small island in the Arickaree River where they dug rifle pits and prepared for a siege. One by one their horses, which were tied to bushes near the pits, were killed until the company was entirely dismounted. Then the savage horde swept in on a furious charge which was meant to end the affair. The Scouts, every one of whom had seen fighting either upon the plains against Indians or in the Civil War, and being armed with new repeating rifles, cooly withstood the onslaught and inflicted heavy losses upon the enemy. Roman Nose was killed in that charge at the head of his warriors. The Indians made two more charges under a new leader but they could neither ride over the island nor drive the Scouts off it. Then they resorted to siege methods.

Five of the scouts were killed, and sixteen, including Lieutenant Colonel Forsyth who was hit three times, were wounded. Among the killed was Surgeon J. H. Mooers. This meant that the wounded got only the crudest kind of medical attention from their comrades. Their food gave out and they had to subsist upon decaying horse flesh. On September 26, nine days after the attack, they were rescued by soldiers from Fort Wallace. Today a tall, square monument stands upon the spot where Ranahan and his comrades fought heroically. For several years after the battle he served as a scout under General E. A. Carr with his old Pony Express comrade, "Buffalo Bill" Cody.

Following his army career he went to Salt Lake City in 1872, and later to Boise, Idaho. Here, in 1877, he married Miss Mary Cullum. After living in Boise many years they moved to Weiser, same state, where they lived on a farm. After Mrs. Ranahan's death in 1914 he moved back to Boise where he died December 27, 1926, at the age of 86 years. During his latter years he delivered many addresses and wrote numerous articles for newspapers on pioneer days and the Indian wars.

RICHARDSON, JOHNSON WILLIAM was one of the first riders hired by Lewis for his Division. He was a native of Virginia and had apparently been to sea, but whether on a merchant ship or in the United States Navy is not known. Documentary evidence bearing upon the question of the identity of the rider who carried the first *mochila* out of St. Joseph, clearly favors Richardson. What he did, and what happened to him after his Pony Express days is not known. Like many another of that band of sturdy, courageous young men, he passed from the scene into complete oblivion.

RISING, DON C. was born in Steuben County, New York in 1844. In 1857 the family migrated to Kansas Territory and built a ranch at the crossing on Log Chain Creek on the Oregon Trail in

Nemaha County. When the Levenworth & Pike's Peak Express Company line was moved north to the route through Julesburg, the ranch became a stage station where mules could be changed and passengers secure a good night's sleep. Later it was also used as a relay station for the Pony Express.

At the age of 16, Rising was hired for Lewis' Division and put on the run between Granada and Marysville. Later he rode from Big Sandy to Fort Kearny. In 1868, after the ponies quit running, he was appointed assistant wagon master in the Union army. During his service he participated in the battles of Island No. 10, Pittsburg Landing, Shiloh, Tuscumbia, and Corinth. Before the war was over he was discharged on account of illness. He next accompanied a wagon train to New Mexico. After his return he engaged in the mercantile and hotel business. From

Courtesy of M. E. Jsmert

Apparently a contemporaneous photograph from an old daguerreotype. Reading from left to right (standing), Billy R i c h a r d s o n, J o h n n y Frye; (seated), Charlie Cliff, and Gus Cliff. These were all riders out of St. Joseph, Missouri.

Pony Express rider Harry L. Roff in later life when he was Pacific manager of Home Insurance Company. He stands at the center between the woman with white blouse and man with whiskers. Roff began service with that company at Virginia City and later became an agent at Oakland. He served as special agent, then district manager, then general agent.

1871 to 1875 he worked as brakeman and conductor on the Missouri Pacific and Santa Fe Railroad. He closed his career as a farmer near Wetmore, Kansas.

ROFF, HARRY L., who was undoubtedly a Pony Express rider, is put forward by a number of writers as the one who carried the first *mochila* to the steamer *Antelope* in San Francisco. The weight of evidence, however, favors James Randall. In later life Roff became an agent for the Home Insurance Company at Virginia City and subsequently moved to Oakland, California, where he was successively appointed Special Agent, District Manager, General Agent, and Pacific Manager for that company.

STREEPER, WILLIAM HENRY was born in Philadelphia, Pennsylvania, August 1, 1837, and later moved to St. Louis, Missouri, with his parents. While living there he got a job lighting the gas street lamps along the river front. He crossed the plains with his family in 1851 and reached Salt Lake City in the fall, where his first work was that of bullwhacker. When he was old enough he set up a freighting business of his own with a line running from Salt Lake City to Los Angeles.

At the time the Central Overland California & Pike's Peak Express Company took over Chorpenning's route, Streeper seems to have been engaged in carrying the "heavy mail," i. e. printed matter too bulky to haul in stage coaches, or on pack mules. Although not a regular Pony Express rider, he probably substituted as such when he was needed. When the Pah Utes put both the Pony Express and his pack mules out of business for a short time in

Courtesy of Charles R. Mabey
William H. Streeper, born Aug. 1, 1837, Philadelphia, Pennsylvania, and died Oct. 8, 1930, Centerville, Utah.

midsummer 1860, he worked for a time as station keeper and assisted Howard Egan in reopening his Division.

When the ponies ran no more he bought two good wagons, a lead one and a trailer, from Russell, Majors & Waddell at Camp Floyd and began freighting from the Missouri River to Salt Lake City. On one of his trips to Omaha the Indians drove off all of his mules, leaving him stranded upon the road. He took an east bound stage back to the city, arranged for more mules, and went on to deliver his cargo in Salt Lake City. He died at Centerville, Utah in October, 1930.

TOPENCE, ALEXANDER was born in Belfort, France, in 1839, and came to America in 1846. The family settled in New York, where Alexander lived until 1854. In that year he went to Missouri with some young friends where he became an employee of Russell, Majors & Waddell as a bullwhacker. He continued in this work until 1858 when he was employed by the Butterfield Overland Mail Company to help establish its line from Missouri to California along the Southern Route. When the Pony Express was started in 1860 he was hired as a rider on Lewis' Division. He also rode on Slade's Division farther west. In 1863 he settled in Salt Lake City and established a freight line to Montana.

TOWNE, GEORGE rode on Lewis' Division between Seneca and Marysville.

TUCKETT, HENRY rode on Howard Egan's Division west of Salt Lake City. He was one of the party organized by Egan to go out along the line to the west in 1860 and put it back into operation after the Indians had disrupted it.

UPSON, WARREN was the son of Lauren Upson, editor of the *Sacramento Union*. He joined the rush of miners to the Washoe mines in Carson Valley, but soon discovered he had no taste for that kind of life. Loving the outdoors, he spent his time on ranches riding horses or in the mountains hunting. He was among the first hired by Bolivar Roberts for his Division and assigned to the run from Sportsman's Hall to Friday's Station on the east side of the Sierra Nevadas.

WALLACE, HENRY was among the initial group hired by Lewis and given the run from Big Sandy to Liberty Farm.

WHALEN, MICHAEL ("MIKE") was born, 1844 in New York City and migrated to St. Joseph, Missouri, about the middle 1850's. At 15 years of age he drove a party of gold seekers from the Missouri River to the infant town of Denver, which at that time consisted of only two adobe houses. On his return he went by way of Omaha, Nebraska.

He was in St. Joseph on April 3, 1860, when he saw the first rider, whom he said was John Frye, take off for the west. That fall he went out along the trail and got a job, probably as stock tender, at one of the stations on Slade's Division. Later, he went to Salt Lake City where in April, 1861, Howard Egan hired him to ride the Pony Express line from that city to Camp Floyd.

After two months service as a rider, the quartermaster at Camp Floyd persuaded him to drive his wife and daughter from Salt Lake City to Fort Leavenworth. After he had done this he enlisted in the United States army. He took part in the battles of Shiloh, Vicksburg Landing, and Corinth. To round out his career as a soldier he marched with Sherman from Atlanta to the sea. After serving three years and twenty days he was discharged. He returned to St. Joseph where he was a grading contractor for many years.

WILSON, ELIJAH NICHOLS ("UNCLE NICK") was born in 1845 and taken to Utah by his parents in 1850. At 9 years of age he was adopted by Chief Washakie's mother, with whom he lived among the Shoshones for about two years. Then he returned to his own family. In 1860, when he was 15 years old, he was hired as a Pony Express rider and put on Egan's Division between Shell Creek and Deep Creek. When his Pony Express days were over he avoided towns and thickly populated areas to live on the frontier. In his latter years he lived in Jackson's Hole, Wyoming, and died near the little town of Wilson, named in his honor, December 26, 1916, age 71 years.

WINTLE, JOSEPH BARNEY was born in 1840. At the age of 20 he was given the run from Fort Kearny to Cottonwood Springs on Lewis' Division. He carried the first *mochila* westward and also President Lincoln's first message to Congress. In accomplishing the latter he rode 110 miles in five hours with ten changes of horses.

On one occasion he met an east bound rider, perhaps Alex Carlyle, who showed him a hole in his hat made by an Indian bullet. In spite of obvious danger that he himself might be attacked if he went on, he finished his run.

Once he was chased for a number of miles by Indians who fired upon him again and again. His grain-fed horse easily outdistanced them, but it cost the life of the horse. Wintle made the next station, but the faithful animal fell dead upon arriving.

One dark night he rode without warning into an Indian camp. With a show of bravery he did not feel he dismounted, handed his reins to a nearby warrior, and entered a lodge. A short time later he came out, gave the warrior a small present, mounted and rode off as though nothing were out of the ordinary.

One day just at dusk he came unexpectedly upon another large Indian encampment. Since he had already been observed, he boldly galloped to the edge of it, dismounted, and pretended to adjust his saddle girth. The Indians did not molest him.

When the Pony Express was disbanded, he engaged in the meat business in Salt Lake City. In 1862 he married Miss Sarah Evans, who was born in England. A year later the young couple started to Wilson, Utah, to establish a home. In fording the Weber River, Mrs. Wintle was drowned. In 1864 he married Miss Marinda Wilson. They made their home at Wilson, 1864-70; Hooper, 1870-75; and in 1902 moved to Ogden. Wintle died there in January, 1916 at 76 years of age.

From these brief sketches it is seen that the Pony Express riders constituted a cosmopolitan group. They were drawn from many walks in life, were the product of almost every type of social environment known in that day, represented a long catalogue of previous vocations, and had their origin in both the New and Old World.

Naturally, many of those hired by J. C. Bromley and Howard Egan for their Divisions were Mormons. It could not have been otherwise. This accounts for those who are listed as having been born in England. They were the sons of converts to that religion and emigrants to Utah.

The age of the riders all along the route is a matter of special interest. Although it was announced in the beginning that 20 was the minimum, an astonishingly large number who were younger were employed. The average for those whose sketches appear here was slightly under 19.

One reason for this was that the job of Pony Express rider was peculiarly adapted to single men. Married men, with the exception of a known few whose homes were in Salt Lake City, did not take to the idea of long separation from their families and life in distant, isolated stations. Since early marriage was the rule on the frontier in those days, this work fell mostly to older teen agers who had not yet assumed martial responsibilities.

From top to bottom, as shown by the ages of those that are known, the Pony Express organization was mostly composed of men in the early prime of life. William H. Russell was 48, Alexander Majors 46, William B. Waddell 53, John W. Russell 24, and Howard Egan 45. It is safe to assume that most of the others whose ages are not known, Division Superintendents, station keepers, and stock tenders, were also younger men.

Here, perhaps, we find the main reason for the increasing popularity of the institution. More than anything else in the history of our country it stands as a glowing symbol of the vision, daring, fortitude, and sheer courage of American youth.

7

STATIONS

Aₗₜₕₒᵤₘ... ALTHOUGH THE SPOT-LIGHT of admiration and praise is usually turned upon the Pony Express riders, their success was impossible without the humble, mostly obscure, and forgotten station keeper and stock tenders. Courage, endurance, and ability to live under the harshest, most primitive of conditions were their primary characteristics. That they did their work well, and were faithful and loyal is evidenced by the remarkable success of the riders. Although only about a third of these are known, it is due them to record their names and that of their stations here.

BADEAU, —————. Badeau's Station on Slade's Division near Fort Laramie.

BERRY, —————. Strawberry Station on Roberts' Division.

BUCKLAND, SAMUEL S. Buckland's Station on Roberts' Division.

CHRISMAN, GEORGE. Julesburg on Lewis' Division.

DUBAIL, CONSTANT. Spring Valley Station on Egan's Division.

ELLSWORTH, RICHARD. Fort Kearny on Lewis' Division.

FAUST, J. H. Faust's or Rush Valley Station on Egan's Division.

GILMAN, —————. Gilman's Station on Slade's Division.

GUENOT, LOUIS. Platte Bridge Station on Bromley's Division.

GUITTARD, GEORGE. Station on Lewis' Division.

RISING, N. H. Log Chain Station on Lewis' Division.

HANKS, EPHRIAM. Big Canyon Station on Egan's Division.

HOLMES, —————. Millersville Station on Bromley's Division.

HOLLENBERG, GEORGE. Hollenberg Station on Lewis' Division.

HOLTON, MIKE. Egan's Station on Egan's Division.

HURST, FREDERICK W. Ruby Valley Station on Egan's Division.

LEWIS, DAVID. Ham's Fork Station on Bromley's Division.

McNAUGHTON, JAMES. Sand Springs Station on Roberts' Division.

MARLEY, W. C. Buckland's Station on Roberts' Division.

Pony Express Leaving Station

MOORE, ————. Three Crossings Station on Bromley's Division.

MYERS, ————. Bear River Station on Bromley's Division.

NEECE, PETER. Willow Creek Station on Egan's Division.

PLANTE, ————. Split Rock Station on Bromley's Division.

REID, WILLIAM A. ("BILL"). Rock Ridge Station on Bromley's Division.

RENI, JULES. Julesburg Station on Lewis' Division.

REYNAL, ————. Spring Valley Station on Roberts' Division.

ROCKWELL, PORTER. Rockwell's Station on Egan's Division.

ROSIER, RALPH. Dry Creek Station on Roberts' Division.

RUSSELL, "HOD." Some station on Slade's Division.

SEVIER, ————. Deep Creek on Roberts' Division.

SMITH; JOHN E. Seneca Station on Lewis' Division.

SMITH, WILLIAM. Nevada Station on Roberts' Division.

THOMAS, ————. Butte Station on Roberts' Division.

TOTTEN, ————. Dry Creek Station on Roberts' Division.

VICKERY, WILLIAM. Syracuse Station on Lewis' Division.

WARD, SETH. Central Star Station on Slade's Division.

WELLMAN, HORACE. Rock Creek Station on Lewis' Division.

WHEELER, ————————. Box Elder Station on Bromley's Division.
WILLIAMS, J. O. Williams Station on Roberts' Division.
WILSON, HENRY. Egan Station on Egan's Division.

Before the Central Overland California & Pike's Peak Express Company was organized, mail stations were in operation between the Missouri River and California. J. M. Hockaday & Company had some between Salt Lake City and Independence, Missouri, at least at Forts Bridger, Laramie, and Kearny. When the Leavenworth & Pike's Peak Express Company took over that line, it established new stage relay stations 25 to 30 miles apart all the way to Salt Lake City. One of the jobs in preparation for the Pony Express was the building of additional stations about half way between the old ones. The latter used *all* stations, but stage coaches stopped only at every other one.

When Chorpenning signed a contract in 1858 to carry the mail from Sacramento to Salt Lake City in stage coaches, he built five stations along Egan's Route about 100 miles apart. As on the line east of Salt Lake City, enough additional stations to accommodate the Pony Express were built. These made the task of opening the new service much easier and in part account for it being accomplished in 65 days.

The location of stations was governed primarily by necessity and not as the convenience or comfort of their occupants might dictate. The distance horses could maintain a grueling pace without injury to them was the determining factor in every case. Since it was believed that this was from 10 to 15 miles, the distance between relay stations was arbitrarily fixed. If this rigid requirement allowed the location of a station upon a desirable spot, it was put there. If not it was placed within those limits regardless even of water and grass. They could haul the one in barrels and drive the horses a reasonable distance to the other.

The pivotal stations along the route were the home stations. These were generally the old stage stations, were better equipped, housed at least two riders, the station keeper, and from two to four stock tenders. Some of them were also home stations for stage drivers. Each marked the end of a rider's run where he met another traveling in the opposite direction. Several spare horses were kept at home stations, as well as supplies and surplus equipment.

The others, known as relay stations, were occupied by the keeper and a stock tender. Their job was to care for the three or four horses stationed there and have one ready, day or night, for the next rider who came along.

From St. Joseph to Fort Kearny, Fort Bridger to Rush Valley, and from Carson City to Sacramento, most of the stations were located in fairly good country and were reasonably comfortable. All others were situated in deserts where conditions were unbelievably harsh and difficult. Some of these were constructed of adobe bricks in the middle of endless, dreary wastes, and others of loose stones in isolated, treeless canyons and unnamed hills. Still others were mere holes dug in the hillside with crude additions in front.

All of them, except those most favorably located, had dirt floors; window glass was unknown; the beds were pole bunks built against the walls, and the furniture consisted of boxes,

Courtesy of Bancroft Library, University of California, Berkeley, California
Pony Express rider, "Overland Pony Express—The Relay Station—Changing Horses" by Bolmar, in Frank Root and Wm. E. Connelley's, *The Overland Stage* (Topeka, Kansas, 1901).

benches, or anything else the ingenuity of the occupants could contrive. Most of them had water nearby, such as it was, and the stable for horses was only a few feet distant from the quarters of the men.

The food provided the stations was not of a quality designed to tickle the palate of an epicurean. It consisted of cured meats, mostly bacon, dried fruits, beans, bread baked upon the spot, molasses, pickles, corn meal when it could be had, and coffee. Fresh meat was a rarity, even in regions where wild animals were numerous, because nobody had time to hunt. Sometimes the wagon trains, which appeared about once a month with supplies, brought along a few delicacies, but these were never plentiful. Those trains also hauled hay and grain for the horses, and space was always at a premium. Nobody thought of stinting *them*, no matter what the cost might be, or how short rations for the men were.

As events quickly proved, the stations in Western Utah and Eastern Nevada were all located in dangerous territory. To the Indians who roamed over those regions, emigration along the Humboldt and the building of stage and Pony Express stations was clear evidence of the white man's intention to take over and settle the country. The situation was critical long before 1860. Therefore, from the day Bolivar Roberts began building stations eastward from Carson City and Howard Egan moved westward from Salt Lake City to meet him, it was inevitable that open warfare should break out.

The station keepers and stock tenders were fully aware of the situation, yet they calmly settled themeselves down in the isolated, practically defenseless little stations along the route. With the exception of home stations every one of them was like a sitting duck which a dozen determined savages could capture at any time.

At St. Joseph those riders whose homes were not in the city lived in Pattee House between runs. In the beginning, when the runs were made only once a week, they had about six days of delightful leisure there every other week. After the service was made bi-weekly they had little time for the sights and pleasures of city life. Short lay-overs for rest was all they got. The St.

"Pony Express and Overland Mail Leaving Smith's Hotel, Seneca, Kans., 1861," by Bolmar in Frank Root and Wm. E. Connelley's, *The Overland Stage,* (Topeka, Kansas, 1901).

Joseph people, after a flurry of excitement at the beginning, seem to have accepted the Pony Express as a matter of course. This was partly due to the fact that after the first run, departures were made at midnight.

Fortunately, the stage line between St. Joseph and Salt Lake City and the Pony Express route throughout its entire length was closely observed by Sir Richard F. Burton, noted English author, traveler, and explorer during the summer and fall of 1860. His account of what he saw and experienced, although quite cynical, critical, and highly prejudiced, constitutes an authentic description of stations, persons, and scenery as they were at that time. He mentions most of the stage stations but omits those used only by the Pony Express.

The first station beyond Elwood, Kansas, was Troy. Next came Cold Springs, a Pony Express relay station. Here lived a family consisting of a mother who cooked the meals, two daughters who served them, and two sons who acted as stock tenders. The surroundings were crude and primitive in the extreme. One could not imagine any woman, except one inured to the limitations of frontier life, living there.

Kennekuk, the first stage and Pony Express relay station west of St. Joseph, boasted a dozen houses, a store, and a blacksmith shop. It was also headquarters for the Kickapoo Indian agent, Major Royal Baldwin. Here the military road from Fort Leavenworth joined that from St. Joseph.

Beyond Kennekuk the route led through a well settled region, with farm houses on the average of a mile apart. The country was rolling, well watered, and pleasing to the eye. Streams were bridged, the road was well traveled, and could not be missed on the darkest night.

Log Chain Station, situated in a grove of beautiful elm, hickory, and walnut trees, was another stage and Pony Express relay station where stage coach passengers might snatch a bit of sleep. It got its name from the fact that the Army of Utah and Russell, Majors & Waddell's wagon trains broke many ox-chains in crossing the creek and left them scattered about in the vicinity. The ranch upon which the station stood was owned by N. H. Rising, station keeper, whose son Don was among the first riders employed by A. E. Lewis for his Division.

Next after Log Chain was Seneca, the first Pony Express home station, 77 miles west of St. Joseph. Levi Hensel, a blacksmith, located here in 1858. Being an expert shoer of horses his fame spread along the stage and Pony Express line, with the result that horses and mules were driven long distances for him to shoe. In the same year John E. Smith built a large two-story house here with lumber hauled from St. Joseph and opened a hotel. The J. M. Hockaday & Company stages stopped there. When the Leavenworth & Pike's Peak Express Company began using this route, it became a stage station and the place was filled with guests almost every night. It was popular with the Pony Express riders because Mrs. Smith set a splendid table and many dances and other entertainments were held. Smith himself was station keeper.

George Guittard kept the station which was known by his name on the Vermilion River. Prior to Pony Express days he had been forced to abandon his journey to California for lack of funds and had settled here. The place was well known from the Missouri River to the Pacific coast. Here, as well as at all stations east of Fort Kearney, the mainstay for food was bacon, eggs, hot rolls and coffee. Sometimes chicken and beef were served, but not often. Vegetables also formed a part of the menu, but the farther west one traveled the more scarce they became.

Marysville, formerly Palmetto City, was a Pony Express relay station housed in the local livery stable. Here the route crossed Big Blue and also the divide between that stream and Little Blue. Then it ascended the latter stream to its source. The valley through which it ran was some two miles wide and bordered on both sides by low, rolling bluffs which were barren of trees. The river bottom was well grassed and covered with flowers of many varieties and hues in summer. The banks of the stream, which were once a favorite grazing ground for numberless buffalo, were bordered with groves of cottonwood.

Hollenberg, or Cottonwood, as it was sometimes called, was a

PONY EXPRESS MARYSVILLE. KANS. 1860

Courtesy of Nebraska State Historical Society

"Marysville Station," by David M. Monrose

Courtesy of John W. Clampitt
James Butler (Wild Bill)
Hickock from John W. Clam-
pitt's "Echoes From the Rocky
Mountains."

J. B. HICKOK. (WILD BILL.)

relay station for both stages and the Pony Express. Here ground had been cleared, plowed, and corn planted. This station was named for the keeper, George Hollenberg, who left his native Germany in 1849 and went to California. In 1852 he went to Australia, and later to Peru in South America. In 1854 he went to Kansas Territory, and three years later established a stage station for J. M. Hockaday & Company upon his ranch.

He erected a large building, the ground floor of which included a store, post-office, kitchen, dining room, and bed room for his family. The six employees stationed there, Pony Express riders and stage drivers, slept in the attic, which extended the entire length of the building. In 1942 this structure was repaired as a Pony Express Memorial and the area around it made into a state park.

After leaving Hollenberg, the road was rough and in the summer clouds of mosquitoes tormented travelers day and night. The next station was Rock Creek, noted as the scene of a gun battle on July 12, 1861, between twenty-three year old James Butler ("Wild Bill") Hickok and David McCanles in which the latter and two other men were killed. This affair, like many other incidents in which Hickok was involved, is highly controversial, with historians of ability differing as to fundamental causes.

Whatever they may have been, it is certain that there was a deep underlying strata of hard feeling between Hickok and McCanles. Some say it was due to rivalry for the affections of a woman who lived near the station, and others to a quarrel between McCanles and Horace Wellman, station keeper, over money due McCanles from the Central Overland California & Pike's Peak Express Company which had bought the station from him on payments.

Regardless of the cause, when the last shot was fired McCanles, James Gordon, and James Wood were dead and Hickok launched upon a career which was to earn him undying notoriety. Hickok and Wellman, both of whom had come through the affray without a scratch, were charged with murder, but were acquitted by a justice of the peace. Hickok later became a scout in the Federal

Pony Express rider, "Pony Express and Overland Mail Office at Fort Kearny, 1861," by Bolmar in Frank Root and Wm. E. Connelley's, *The Overland Stage* (Topeka, Kansas, 1901).

army, Indian fighter, and frontier peace officer. He was killed, shot from behind, by Jack McCall in Deadwood, South Dakota, August 2, 1876. Wild Bill is credited by some as being a Pony Express rider, but it is doubtful that he ever was anything more than a stock tender.

In 1860 the valley of the Little Blue was devoid of animal life. Twenty years before, it teemed with buffalo, wild horses, turkeys, and every other form of prairie life. Immigrants and hunters drove the game away and the country was as lonely as the Sahara desert. Buffalo were now found only far away, wild horses had disappeared, and turkeys were unknown.

At Liberty Farm both stage coach mules and Pony Express horses were changed. Further on was Thirty-Two Mile Station where lived a family of Vermonters. Nearby was a trading post which was frequented by soldiers from Fort Kearny. Some forty miles beyond this was Valley Station, a home and relay station. In this neighborhood the aspect of the country began to change and signs of approaching the desert began to appear.

Fort Kearney, which was a United States post office, was merely a stopping place for stages and Pony Express riders, the former

PONY EXPRESS RIDERS CHANGING HORSES ENROUTE FROM NEVADA TO CALIFORNIA

"Changing Horses" by Ted McFall, Reno, Nevada: Four color painting on glass. This painting is one of hundreds on the walls of the main floor of Harold's Club. All the paintings deal with early Nevada and Western history.

to pick up passengers and the latter any letters that might be awaiting them. Not many months after the Express started a telegraph line from Omaha reached here.

The next station, reached over a road filled with chuck holes caused by rivulets running across it, was Seventeen Mile, where both stage drivers and Pony Express riders changed animals.

Plum Creek boasted a landlady, the wife of the station keeper. Here Sir Richard F. Burton met buffalo steaks for the first time and found little to praise in them. He complained that it was the driest meat he ever tasted and had to grease it with pork fat in order to be able to swallow it. Midway, a relay station, also had a landlady.

Gilman's, being only a Pony Express relay station, was not a stage stop. Here, William Campbell, employed by the company in 1860 to help supply stations and to become an express rider later in the year met his bride to be. Campbell was the last survivor of that band of courageous young men who carried the *mochilas* over the long trail.

Along here the valley of the South Platte was a broad prairie with hills and bluffs along the river bottom. Trees were plentiful and dwarf cedars began to appear. Cottonwood Station had one small room where travelers slept upon pallets on the floor. That is, they slept if they could. Beyond this point the Platte spread out into wide basins and lagoons filled with flags and water-rushes. On the west side of the valley was a range of buttes composed of red, sandy clay which ended in perpendicular bluffs at the edge of the valley.

The station at Fremont Spring, which was composed of two buildings with a roofed-over space between them, was kept by a man and his wife. He received $30 per month for his services and in the summer of 1860 she was attempting to establish a flock of chickens.

O'Fallon's Bluffs, Elkhorn, or Halfway House, as it was variously known, was in a trading post. Here a sign informed the wayfarer that he was now 400 miles from St. Joseph, 120 from Fort Kearny, 68 from the Upper and 40 from the Lower Crossing of the South Platte.

Julesburg, a cluster of unpainted shacks, at the Upper California Crossing on the South Platte, was the most noted station on the whole route in 1860. The place was famous from earliest days because fording the river here was always a difficult, dangerous undertaking. Emigrants looked forward to that experience with dread and when it was over they remembered it with gratitude, providing they had no trouble.

The place got its name from Jules Reni, a wild, whiskey guzzling French-Canadian trapper and Indian trader who established a ranch and trading post there. It was first known as "Jules' Ranch," then "California Crossing," but people got to calling it "Julesburg," and the name stuck. It sticks to this day too.

Being located far from civilization it became headquarters for a lawless crowd of horse thieves, highwaymen, and shady characters in general. When the Leavenworth & Pike's Peak Express Company was transferred from the original route to the Oregon Trail early in the summer of 1859, Beverley D. Williams appointed "Old Jules," as everyone called him, station keeper.

Later developments proved that the wrong man had been appointed to that place. From the first day coaches rolled over the line horses and other property regularly disappeared. By the time the Central Overland California & Pike's Peak Express Company was organized, in October, 1859, the situation had become intolerable. Thieves had become bolder, thefts of horses more numerous, and stage schedules were sometimes disrupted. At this time Benjamin F. Ficklin succeeded Williams. One of the first jobs he had to do was clean up the line.

Ficklin was just the man needed for the job. Since nobody with authority to keep the peace and restrain criminals was nearer than Forts Kearny and Laramie or Denver, stage company officials had to take matters into their own hands. Consequently Ficklin committed the job of cleaning up the line from Julesburg to South Pass to Division Superintendent Joseph A. Slade.

No better choice could have been made. Slade was a native of Carlyle, Illinois, and came of a respectable family. The story goes that in 1842, at the tender age of 13, he killed his first man, an old German whose privy he and other boys had overturned.

Angered by the man's understandably irate language and a blow from his cane, Slade hurled a stone at him. The missile went true, struck the German in the temple and killed him.

That night he started for Texas, a favorite hiding place for fugitives from the law. There he finished growing up and served in the War with Mexico under a Captain Killman. One day he led a detail upon a dangerous reconnaissance. Before it returned the number of men he had killed rose to ten.

After the war he married a beautiful girl by the name of Virginia, whom he called "Molly," and engaged in the freighting business. Later he drifted to Western Missouri where he worked at the same job for a company with headquarters at St. Joseph. While on a trip through Wyoming he shot Andrew Farrar, a friendly companion in a drinking bout, who dared him to shoot. Filled with remorse at what he had done, Slade sent a messenger to Fort Bridger for a doctor, but Farrar died. Somewhere and somehow he acquired the title of "Captain," and insisted upon being addressed as such.

Slade was the kind of a man J. M. Hockaday & Company needed on its mail route. He was trailwise, experienced, devoid of fear, and highly expert with guns, especially revolvers. The date upon which he went to work for that company is not known, but when the Leavenworth & Pike's Peak Express Company bought it in 1858, Slade went along with it as Division Superintendent between Julesburg and South Pass.

Having known all the time that Jules' Ranch was headquarters for the outlaws and riff-raff of the frontier, and suspecting that Reni himself was the leader of the gang, Slade's first act was to discharge him. This so infuriated the old trapper that he waylaid Slade and shot him with a double-barrelled shot-gun loaded with buckshot.

Not long afterward Ficklin came along on a stage, heard what had happened, seized Old Jules, hanged him, then rode calmly on. Before he was out of sight friends of Jules cut him down, thereby saving his life.

Slade went to St. Louis, had the buckshot extracted from his body, and came back. In the meantime Old Jules and his gang left Julesburg and established themselves near Rocky Ridge east of South Pass.

Gathering together half a dozen or so men of his own type Slade renewed his campaign with zeal. First, he went to Fort Laramie and explained the state of affairs to army officers stationed there. They agreed with him that drastic action was necessary. Having gotten a clearance of sorts, he set out to run down Old Jules.

He ran his quarry to earth at Pacific Springs, west of South Pass. Calvin Downs, one of the Pony Express riders, said Old Jules fled on horseback and that Slade knocked him from the saddle with a bullet through the hips. After tying the wounded man to the snubbing post in a corral his captor cooly practiced pistol shooting with him as the target. When Old Jules was dead, Slade cut off both his ears, nailed one to the post as a warning to other thieves, and carried its mate in his pocket.

They ran a rancher out of the country because he sold the stage company a stack of hay which had been built upon a large brush-pile, and burned the buildings of others who were suspected of stealing horses. They rode to the hangout of four men who were accused of robbing a stage coach. Slade kicked the door open and walked in, guns blazing. He killed three of them but the fourth crawled through a broken window and got outside. A bullet from Slade's gun brought him down before he had run a hundred yards. So it went from day to day up and down the Division. He forbade bar tenders to sell liquor to stage company employees and shot one who dared to defy him. Within a few months his Divison was rid of its menacing outlaws.

Slade's exploits in cleaning up the stage line gained him such a fearful reputation that his very name was enough to hold criminals in check. When Ben Holladay took over the Central Overland California & Pike's Peak Express Company and opened a new stage line through Souhtern Wyoming in 1862, Slade built a new station near the Colorado-Wyoming line and called it Virginia Dale in honor of Molly. Division headquarters was established there. It was a beautiful place, with commodious buildings and a little stream running through it. In 1865 a traveler who saw it observed two imitation cannon made of stovepipe to awe the Indians.

According to the scant testimony recorded by a few who came into intimate contact with him, Slade was courteous, kind, and obliging when sober. When drunk he was rowdy, destructive, and dangerous to friend and foe alike.

On one occasion, while living at Virginia Dale, he appeared in Denver, took a few drinks, then began to indulge in his favorite pastime of wrecking saloons. When word of this reached the company office, David Street, paymaster, whom Slade admired and liked very much, set out to round him up. Not recognizing his friend, Slade wounded him severely. When informed next day of what he had done his remorse knew no bounds. He refused to go home, stayed sober, and remained by Street's bedside until he was well on the road to recovery. After he had gone on a spree of that kind he always made the rounds to pay for any damage he had done.

As might have been expected, he went too far at last. While traveling along the line in Southern Wyoming with several of his men, they stopped at the sutler's store at Fort Halleck. After a few drinks they started a fight with a number of soldiers who were also drinking. When it was over several of the soldiers had been hurt and the place was a shambles. The commandant at the Fort, having had experience with Slade before, demanded that the company discharge him. This was done, and his service with Ben Holladay's stage line was over.

Robert Spotswood of Denver, who was appointed to succeed him, went to Virginia Dale to take over the business. After a good dinner prepared by Molly, Spotswood broke the news. Slade, being sober, took it calmly, and obligingly made up an inventory of company property. Within a few days he left for Fort Bridger, where he lived for a short time.

In the summer of 1863 H. S. Gilbert, a prominent Utah trader and merchant, hired him to take a wagon train of supplies to Virginia City, Montana. He made the trip successfully, and liked the country so well that he located at a ranch on Meadow Creek in the Madison Valley some twelve miles from that city. Molly joined him here. They built a small house, called the place "Spring Dale," and made their home there.

Here began the period of his life which has supplied material for a controversy that has lasted almost a century. The Montana gold region of that day presented the roughest, wildest scene ever known in American history. Thirty thousand miners and twelve towns were jammed into a narrow, twelve mile long Alder Gulch. All of the characteristic factors in the makeup of the early mining town were found there in abundance.

Henry Plummer was elected sheriff of Virginia City, but the situation grew steadily worse. Highway robbery and murder were common everyday affairs. Early in 1864 the Vigilantes, who went to work in earnest, were organized. Having learned that Plummer was the leader of the worst gang of criminals in the region they seized him and twenty of his men and hanged them at the town of Bannack.

When Slade settled down at Spring Dale he lived quietly for a time. Then, becoming restless, he spent more and more time in town. There he repeated his old stunt of taking a few drinks and wrecking saloons. When the Vigilantes set up a Miner's Court to try law breakers, Slade was arrested and brought in. He contemptuously tore up the warrant for his arrest and threatened the judge with a revolver. That was a fatal error. He was again seized, tried by a Vigilante Committee and this time sentenced to be hung.

He plead for his life and promised to leave the country. But nobody listened. Prominent citizens, including the judge of the Miner's Court whom he had defied, interceded for him but without success. One of Slade's friends raced out to Spring Dale to bring Molly in. When she arrived on an exhausted horse his body was lying under a blanket in the Virginia Hotel.

Was Slade an outlaw and road agent? That is what the controversy is all about. Thomas J. Dimsdale, who wrote a book on the Montana Vigilantes, said he was a member of the group which hung him. Arthur H. Chapman, author of *The Pony Express*, 1932, says that officials of the Overland Stage Company with whom he discussed Slade's character said no Division on the whole line was better run than his and that the sole reason for his discharge was his wild, drunken sprees. On the other hand Calvin Downs and other riders on the Julesburg-South Pass Division said that he held up their pay. "Pony Bob" Haslam, messenger on Wells, Fargo & Company Salt Lake City-Virginia line, who saw him hanged, said he thereby got his "come-uppance" for cheating the boys.

Slade was buried at Bannack, but within a year Molly got permission to move his body to Illinois. Instead of taking it there she hauled it to Salt Lake City and buried it in the old Mormon cemetery. Thus perished a man who is credited with having killed almost 30 of his fellows. If all of the facts concerning his extraordinary career are ever brought to light, it is possible that he may be enshrined beside Wild Bill Hickok, Bill Masterson, Wyatt Earp, and others of their kind.

8

STATIONS (continued)

LODGE POLE CREEK, the first station beyond Julesburg, was part a dugout in a hillside. The mud walls were papered with pages from *Harper's Weekly, Frank Leslie's Weekly*, and the *New York Illustrated News*. The beds were mere bunks, and boxes served as chairs. Beside the door upon a bench was a tin wash basin, a bucket of water, and a public towel.

Mud Springs, which got its name from a small rivulet nearby, was constructed of sod, with an open shed beside it. Since no sleeping quarters were provided for travelers, they had to bed down where they could. Sir Richard F. Burton's bedroom the night he stopped there was an empty wagon box.

Scott's Bluffs, with Robidou's Fort nestling at the base, was a landmark known to all who traveled that way. The distance was 285 miles from Fort Kearny and 51 from Fort Laramie. From the distance the bluffs resembled a blue mound, but upon nearer approach took on the aspect of a medieval walled city. The station here was a Pony Express relay station.

Spring Ranch was kept by a French-Canadian by the name of Reynal who had a squaw for a wife and a pretty half-breed daughter. He had been an Indian trader in his youth, a prisoner among the Pawnees, and later an adopted son of that tribe.

Badeau's Ranch was kept by another French-Canadian by that name. His establishment, which boasted a store and a number of cabins, was also known as "Laramie City."

The station at Fort Laramie was merely an office for both stage and Pony Express. No mules or horses were kept here.

Beyond Fort Laramie there were two roads, one running along the Plate River, which was favored by emigrants, and the other near the Black Hills. The latter, being somewhat shorter, was used by the stage coaches and Pony Express. Ward's or Central Star west of Fort Laramie was a relay station for both stage drivers and Pony Express riders.

Horseshoe Station, the most pretentious between Julesburg and Sacramento, was the home of Division Superintendent, Joseph A. Slade. Women travelers were allowed to sleep indoors, but as elsewhere, men slept out of doors where they pleased or in the stable upon the hay. Slade's wife, Molly, whom Burton characterized as "cold and disagreeable in manner, full of proper pride, with a touch-me-not air" was mistress of the household. Another woman, a disciple of Mrs. Amelia Jenks Bloomer, also lived there.

In August, 1860, owing to a change in the route, nothing had been built at La Bonte Station except a corral for mules and horses. The station keeper and stock tender were living in a brush arbor. Box Elder, kept by a man named Wheeler, was the next station.

At Deer Creek the Indian Agent, Major Twiss, had his headquarters. Here was a post-office, store, and saloon. The latter was owned by an old Indian trader by the name of Bisonette. Ten miles farther on was Little Muddy, built of stones laid up without mortar. The only furniture in the place was a box and a trunk.

Platte Bridge Station was near a toll bridge over the North Platte. It was built about 1859 by Louis Guenot, station keeper,

Courtesy of Archives and Western History Department, University of Wyoming Library
"Deer Creek Station," by C. Moellman

Courtesy of Archives and Western History Department, University of Wyoming Library
"Sweetwater Station" by C. Moellman

at a cost of $40,000. The buildings were comfortable and the traveler, weary with primitive living along the trail, could find rest and refreshment here. Ten miles beyond was Red Butte Station, so-called because of red bluffs nearby. Willow Springs, whose buildings consisted merely of a small rough structure with no corral, was next. It was a home and relay station for stages and Pony Express riders.

In the summer of 1860 Sweetwater Station had been abandoned for some reason, which made Split Rock the next stop. On the way one passed Independence Rock, a peculiar formation not unlike the back of a huge monster 1000 feet long, 400 to 500 feet wide, and 60 to 100 feet high. Upon its surface was inscribed the names of a multitude of people who had traveled past it.

Beyond Independence Rock was Devil's Gate, a gorge 250 yards long, 40 to 105 feet wide, and 300 to 400 feet deep, through which the Sweetwater River foamed. A French-Canadian by the name of Plante kept the station at Split Rock.

Near Independence Rock the road left the North Platte, and entered the valley of the Sweetwater River. This stream, said Burton, was "a perfect Naiad of the mountains." The station keepers, stage drivers, and Pony Express riders affectionately spoke of it as "her," and the tinkling of its waters was music to the ear after having been associated with the gloomy, silent Platte.

The fame of Mrs. Moore, wife of the station keeper at Three Crossings, home station for stage drivers and Pony Express riders, as an excellent housekeeper and cook had traveled far along the route. Both she and her husband were Mormon emigrants from England. When she heard that many men in Utah had more than one wife, she refused to continue her journey to Salt Lake City.

Principal landmarks beyond Three Crossings included the famous Ice Slough, where ice a few inches below a layer of soil and heavy grass, was found the year round. Nearby was Warm Springs. Beyond these the country was sterile, barren, and hopeless. Rock Creek station was as desolate as the country in which it was located.

When travelers reached South Pass they felt they had accomplished something noteworthy. And they had, in those slow motion days. Here was a well built ranch kept by two French-Canadians. Nearby was South Pass City. South Pass was in reality not a pass, but a wide level plain slightly tilted up on edge. So gentle is the eastern slope that one scarcely knows he is climbing to higher altitude. Two miles beyond the Continental Divide was Pacific Springs where relays for both stages and Pony Express were kept. The building was a small log shanty with boards placed upon boxes for seats.

Next was Dry Sandy, kept by a young Mormon and his wife. Beyond was Simpson's Hollow where the Mormons captured a Russell, Majors & Waddell wagon train under Lewis Simpson in 1857.

Green River, which was a home station for both stage drivers and Pony Express riders, was something of a settlement. It boasted a grocery and other stores and a ferryboat which was used to cross Green River when it was at flood. Its immediate surroundings had the appearance of an oasis in a desert, although almost all the trees in the vicinity had been cut down by imigrants. Three English women, two married and one single, lived here. Between

Green River and the next station was a trading post operated by Michael Martin, a French-Canadian, who sold liquor, linens, ribbons, calico, jams, preserves, buckskin clothes, moccasins, etc. A short distance beyond was the spot where the Mormons got two more of Russell, Majors & Waddell's wagon trains in 1857.

Ham's Fork was kept by David Lewis, a Scotch Mormon who was the husband of two sisters and the father of a platoon of children. The road from here led past a spot which was thickly strewn with the bones of Russell, Majors & Waddell's cattle which had died of cold, overwork, and starvation in 1857.

At Millersville the station was kept by a man named Holmes who also operated a trading post. The place was named after A. B. Miller, partner of William H. Russell and William B. Waddell in the firm of Miller, Russell & Company which opened a store here in 1857. Holmes was a Mormon with a pretty wife from England. The station, corral fences, and furniture were all constructed of parts of abandoned wagon boxes from Russell, Majors & Waddell's wagon trains. Nearby stood a long row of the vehicles, A few miles beyond Millersville was "Uncle Jack" Robinson's trading establishment of seven Indian lodges. He was an old hand at the business and in the course of thirty-four years in the west had accumulated a fortune of $75,000 which was invested in St. Louis property.

There was no stage or Pony Express station at Fort Bridger because land for the grazing of horses and mules could not be obtained on the government reservation. General A. S. Johnston's Army of Utah set up winter quarters here, 1857-58, and called the place Camp Scott. With only a brief halt at the Sutler's store and post office, which were operated by Judge W. A. Carter, stages and Pony Express riders hurried on.

Another French-Canadian, who was the husband of an English woman, kept the station at Muddy Creek. Accommodations here were good, but there was no store. Beyond this the country was a broken land of spurs, hollows, and canyons with a heavy growth of fir and pine. The road led along the crest of a rise, which extended to Quaking Asp. Passing on through an incredibly rough

Pony Express Station

and tortured region the traveler reached Bear River Valley. This stream, one of the principal affluents of Great Salt Lake, flowed in a slightly northwest direction until reaching the noted Beer Spring, where it turned abruptly to the southwest.

Bear River station, standing in a half mile wide bottom, was kept by a Mormon whose name was Myers. He was living with his fifth wife, having divorced the previous four. Burton found him studying a copy of Volney's *Ruins of Empire* and eager to discuss politics, both ancient and modern.

Passing Needle Rocks Station the road entered Echo Canyon whose remarkable formations and red walls rose 300 to 400 feet into the air. Through it wound Weber River, its banks lined with trees, willows, grass and other vegetation. In 1853 the stone building, which later became Weber stage and Pony Express station was erected at its mouth. The following year James E. Bromley settled there and was put in charge of W. M. F. McGraw's mail route from Independence, Missouri, to Salt Lake City. Hiram Kimball got the contract in 1856, but the service was cut off when Johnston's army marched to Utah.

When service was resumed early in 1858, S. B. Miles first had the contract. Later a new one was made with J. M. Hockaday & Company for a weekly service in four-mule wagons or coaches. Bromley worked for Miles and also for Hockaday. When the Leavenworth & Pike's Peak Express Company bought out the latter, he continued with it. In 1860 he became Division Superintendent for the Central Overland California & Pike's Peak Express Company. When the Pony Express was put into operation he stocked the line, hired riders, and built stations as far east as Fort Laramie.

In 1860 Weber Station was only partially built, but it was a very important one with considerable activity. In the summer and fall a large amount of wild hay was cut and stacked for use there and at other stations along the line. The station house was comfortable and well supplied with vegetables raised by Mormons who lived nearby. Beyond it was Carson House Station, kept by two young Mormons. The building was so new in the latter part of the summer of 1860 that doors and windows had not yet been installed. The next was Dixie Creek, where Pony Express horses were changed. Beyond it was the steep ascent of Big Mountain from whose summit the traveler had his first view of Great Salt Lake.

Big Canyon, or Snyder's Mill, stood at the western base of Big Mountain. The keeper was one of the noted trio of Mormon Danites, Ephriam Hanks, a kinsman of President Lincoln. Seventeen miles further on, across Little Mountain and through Emigration Canyon, the road led into Salt Lake City. Salt Lake House on Main Street was a home station where stage drivers and Pony Express riders laid over until their next run.

When the Chorpenning contract was turned over to the Central Overland California & Pike's Peak Express Company, March 20, 1860, weekly stage coaches were running between Salt Lake City and Sacramento. The Pah Ute War broke up this service and when Burton passed over the line in August of that year it had not yet been resumed. The mail going that way was carried by pack mules.

West of Salt Lake City the route, as far as Carson City, was in many respects quite different from that east of it. Upon leaving the city it ran between the Wasatch Mountains and the River Jordan. As it proceeded southward the country became more rugged and barren.

The first station boasted the deceptive title, "Traveler's Rest." After it came Rockwell's, named after another of the noted Danites, Porter Rockwell. Next was Joe's Dugout, which stood at the foot of a steep road leading over the divide between Jordan and Cedar Valleys. It was what its name implied, a mere dugout in a hillside, with a split cedar roof and an adobe chimney. Joe had gone to the trouble of digging a well over a hundred feet deep, but found the soil as dry at the bottom as it was at the top. Consequently water was hauled to the station in barrels.

Camp Floyd was established in beautiful Cedar Valley by General A. S. Johnston in 1858. In 1860 Colonel P. St. George Cooke with two or three hundred men occupied it. When the Civil War broke out the garrison was ordered east and the place abandoned.

After Pass Station came Faust's or Rush Valley, over which J. H. ("Doc") Faust presided. Beyond it was Point Lookout, which was the doorway to the worst desert on the North American Continent. Ahead lay a country of bare, rocky mountain ranges, limitless miles of parched sand, scant herbage, dust storms, shimmering mirages in summer and deadly cold in winter. It was a lonely land and devoid of civilized habitations. Even wild animals seemed to shun it. Since life along this route was extremely rugged, none of the gentler sex were found at the stations on it.

From Camp Floyd to Roberts Creek, some 300 miles to the west, the road followed what was known to the Mormons as "Egan's Route," first explored by Howard Egan in 1853. In 1855 he again traveled it on mule back to win a wager that he could make the trip from Salt Lake City to Sacramento in ten days. This route was that chosen by Chorpenning for his mail line in 1858. He erected five stations upon it and put Egan in charge of the line.

When the Pony Express was started Egan was made Division

Pony Express Station, Fish Springs

Superintendent of that part of it extending from Salt Lake City to Roberts Creek. He built new stations, hired riders, stock tenders, and station keepers. At least two horses for riders were kept at all of them, as well as mules for the stage and mail line.

At Fish Springs, whose water was filled with small, perch-like fish, two men had charge of the usual number of horses and mules. The water was warm and had a sulphurous taste, but those who lived there had become accustomed to it. Along the road for many miles past this place the ground was so thickly encrusted with alkali that it looked like snow.

Boyd's Station, which consisted of a single room log hut, was next. Then came Willow Creek, the scene of Peter Neece's fight with the Pah Utes in June, 1860. Deep Creek Canyon was a nine mile long gorge which afforded countless opportunities for ambush by Indians that summer. At its western end was Deep Creek ranch and station, owned by Howard Egan. The buildings consisted of a station house, a large dwelling of adobe bricks, and two smaller ones used for sleeping and cooking. Hay, grain, and livestock for the Pony Express and stage line were produced here. The station keeper was a Mormon by the name of Sevier. Nearby on a government reservation lived a band of peaceable Gosh Ute Indians.

In June, 1860, the Indians burned the Antelope Springs Station and as late as October it had not been rebuilt. The keeper of the next station, Spring Valley, was Constant Dubail, a Frenchman. It was here that Elijah N. Wilson was wounded in the head by an arrow.

Egan's Station, situated in a canyon of that name, gained fame in October, 1860, when Lieutenant Weed's Dragoons appeared upon the scene in the nick of time to prevent 80 Gosh Utes from roasting Mike Holton and another man alive at the stake.

Butte Station, locally known as "Robber's Roost," was kept by a Mormon from England by the name of Thomas. The building, some thirty feet long, was built of stones with mud between them. The door was the rear end of a wagon box bearing bullet marks. The inside was divided into two rooms by a canvas partition. One of these was provided with two bunks for four men. Beneath them were rubbish, harness, saddles, sacks of wheat, oats, meal, and potatoes. In fact the room did double duty as a bed and storage room.

The other room had a spring under one corner of the wall and a huge fireplace. The furniture consisted of log benches, three legged stools, and a large table made of rough planks. Upon a smaller one near the fireplace was a tin coffee pot, iron knives, forks, and pewter spoons. Upon pegs driven into the wall were hung clothing, spurs, quirts, rifles, and revolvers. A shelf beside the door held a tin bucket, wash basin, and a tin can for a dipper.

Ruby Valley, some fifty miles east of Roberts Creek, was considered the half-way point between Salt Lake City and Sacramento. A farm, maintained by the Indian Bureau of Utah Territory was located here. It was under the supervision of William ("Uncle Billy") Roberts, assistant Indian Agent, and was intended to teach the Red Men how to become farmers. Chokup, chief of a band of some 500 Gosh Utes, lived here.

Diamond Spring, with its warm clear water was next, and after it Roberts Creek. The station was burned by the Indians in midsummer, 1860, and had not been fully rebuilt as late as October. Several Indians acted as stock tenders here, for which they received one square meal a week. One of the employees here was a young Pennsylvanian who found a cure for his tuberculosis in the desert country.

Dry Creek Station, with the graves of Ralph Rosier and John Applegate nearby, was under the supervision of a man named Totten when it was reopened after the Pah Ute War. Since it had no accommodations for travelers, Burton slept in a haystack the night he stopped there.

At Simpson's Park, James Alcott was killed, the station burned, and the stock driven off during the Pah Ute War. Two Indians were employed here to herd the stock. Another of the employees was Giovanni Brutisch. Reese River Station, which was also destroyed, was being rebuilt in October.

Smith's Creek Station, which came through the Pah Ute War unscathed, was kept by two Irishmen from New York and a Mexican by the name of Antoine who was an old express rider on the San Bernardino trail.

Cold Springs, which was also destroyed, lacked a roof in Oc-

Courtesy of Charles Kelley

"Mountain Dell Station" by Dan Weggeland

tober. It was a home station. Williams Station was kept by J. O. Williams with two of his brothers as stock tenders. The latter and three other men were killed there on May 7, 1860. This was the incident which started the Pah Ute War.

Buckland's Station was called Fort Churchill after that post was built there in the summer of 1860. Carson City Station was located in the first town west of Salt Lake City. Being the largest in the Carson River Valley it was the metropolis of the mining region known as the "Washoe Mines." Friday's Station, located at the foot of Lake Tahoe, was well known in Pony Express days. Strawberry which had nothing to do with that well known fruit, was so called because travelers said that the keeper, a man named Berry, fed their horses straw instead of the hay for which they were charged.

Although these glimpses of the route, stations upon it, and the people who lived in them are necessarily brief and incomplete, they serve as an index to things as they were in those long-gone days. They also serve to emphasize the magnitude of the undertaking and the quality of the men who made a conspicuous success of it.

9

THE PAH UTE WAR

THE HISTORY of the American frontier as it
advanced westward from the Atlantic seaboard
was, with few exceptions, a story of conflict with Indians. One
reason for this was the obvious fact that the appearance of white
men, such as the early trappers and hunters, even in small numbers, introduced sweeping changes, not for the better, into the
Red Man's simple, primitive way of life.

The Indians, having occupied the country for generations before the white man appeared, naturally felt it belonged to
them. The white men, totally disregarding Indian claims and
recognizing no previous ownership whatever, took it over by
force. It was a simple, tragic situation, yet one fraught with fateful
consequences for both.

As early as 1832, when George Nidiver's party of trappers encountered hostile Shoshones along the Humboldt River in what
is now the State of Nevada, the Indians resented the intrusion of
white men into the plains and mountains west of Great Salt Lake.

The rush of gold seekers to California in 1849 and subsequent
years troubled the Indians greatly. In that year several trains
were attacked on the Humboldt River and their cattle taken. A
pursuing party was made up from trains following and thirty of
the assailants killed. During the summer of 1850 there was constant skirmishing in Carson Valley to the southwest in the neighborhood of Lake Tahoe between emigrants and Indians. For half
a dozen years afterward deeds of violence by both emigrants and
Indians were numerous on the Humboldt.

In 1858 Old Winnemucca, as he was known, a friend of the
white people and head chief of the Pah Utes in the Honey Lake

region, made a treaty with the settlers there under which aggressors of both groups were punished for acts of violence. He took his warriors into battle of the side of the whites and helped drive the Pit River Indians out of the country. When the Washoes raided the Roop County potato fields, his warriors rode with the retaliatory white men. One of them was killed in a skirmish and the Pah Utes believed a white man fired the shot. When the murder of Peter Lassen, 1853, was charged to his people Winnemucca became angry.

The winter of 1859-60 was an exceptionally severe one during which the Pah Utes, who numbered about 6,000 in the Carson district in Western Nevada, suffered intensely. In spite of their plight and the death of many children, their hatred and distrust of white men were so great they would not receive offerings of food for fear it was poisoned. To their simple, savage minds their tragic misfortunes were due to the presence of white people in their country.

In January, 1860 the Pah Utes killed Dexter E. Deming on Willow Creek north of Honey Lake. Governor Isaac Roop, head of the provisional government of the new Territory of Nevada, ordered a detachment of Captain William Weatherlow's Rangers under Lieutenant J. W. Tutt to pursue them. This they did, but without results. Captain Weatherlow himself and Thomas J. Harvey were appointed commissioners to deal with the Indians. They demanded the surrender of those who had killed Deming only to be met by refusal on the part of Winnemucca. Not only that, the chief demanded $16,000 as payment for Honey Lake Valley into which white men had intruded.

In the latter part of April the Pah Utes held a council at Pyramid Lake in which they recited their grievances. Among them was the invasion of their hunting grounds and the cutting down of pinon nut trees, both of which were important sources of food supply.

Every chief in the council, with the exception of Numaga, known as Young Winnemucca, but not related to the head chief, was in favor of war. Since he had associated considerably with white men, he understood their power better than any of the others. Winnemucca secretly supported the war faction, for reasons of policy said he would be governed by the majority. Present in the council were a Shoshone chief and a half-breed Bannack by the name of Mogoannoga, both of whom were eager to fight.

Meanwhile the Pony Express route was laid out, the stations built, and the line put into operation. Among those stations was Williams Station about ten miles northeast of Buckland's. J. O. Williams, and two of his brothers, David and Oscar operated it. Samuel Sullivan, James Fleming and another man by the name of Dutch Phil were stopping there in the early part of May, 1860.

Just what happened at this juncture has long been a matter for debate. Certain it is, however, that Mogoannoga stole away from the council at Pyramid Lake with a small party of warriors. Some say he had become impatient with delay and set out to strike a blow which would initiate war. Others, following the account of William Wright ("Dan Dequille"), editor of the *Territorial Enterprise* at Virginia City, Nevada, tell a different story.

He said, fourteen years later, that in the absence of J. O. Williams from the station, two or three young men captured two Pah Ute women and held them prisoners in a nearby cave for several days. The husband of one of them traced the captives to the station but was driven away when he went to rescue his wife. He then approached Mogoannoga who got together a party of warriors and set out for Williams station.

The one point of agreement here is that Mogoannoga rounded up a party of fighting men and took to the warpath. The immediate cause therefore is incidental. On May 7 they crept up to the station in a surprise attack and killed David and Oscar Williams as they stood outside the building talking. They got Sullivan as he fled for his life. Fleming and Dutch Phil were killed inside the station.

The Pah Ute War was on. After burning the building to the ground the raiders set off down the trail toward the west, driving off W. H. Bloomfield's cattle as they went along. Buckland's

Station was their destination, but at sunup they changed their minds and headed for Pyramid Lake. To make certain of a royal welcome they sent one of the party on ahead to announce their coming.

At the council Young Winnemucca was doing his best to avert conflict with the white men. When he saw no one would listen to his pleas for peace he threw himself upon the ground where he lay for three days fasting. Then he reappeared in the council and spoke passionately for the last time.

He warned them that they could not win, many of them would be killed, and the survivors driven into the desert to perish of starvation. As he finished, the messenger from Mogoannoga rode in and reported the attack on Williams station. The council immediately broke up and its members prepared for war.

J. O. Williams returned to his station on the morning of May 8, saw what had happened, and set out to the west for Virginia City to sound the alarm. His report fanned the smothering coals of hatred for the Indians into searing flames. Messengers were sent in every direction to warn prospectors and isolated communities of their danger but for some of them it was too late. On the day of the raid upon Williams Station, settlers were attacked at Honey Lake; John Gibson and seven others were killed sixty miles away, and two more on Truckee River.

At Virginia City, Carson City, Genoa, and Gold Hill the people were stirred to action. Volunteers in varying numbers from all these marched to Buckland's where 105 were organized into companies. Among those from Carson City was Bartholomew Riley, honorably discharged from Company E, 19th United States Cavalry at Camp Floyd a short time before, who had stopped there on his way to California to join his family.

After burying the five men at Williams Station, they proceeded to Truckee River on the night of the 11th. Here they found five men who had been fighting Indians for several days. They said three of their companions had been killed before they reached that stream. On the 12th they moved on up the Truckee.

It appears that Major William O. Ormsby was the nominal

leader of the expedition, but he could hardly be said to have been in command of it. Actually, nobody seems to have had any authority over the several groups comprising it. The volunteers held a deep-rooted contempt for the Pah Utes as fighters. Therefore the march resolved itself into something of a lark. They were brave enough, but this attitude, plus inffective arms, and total lack of military leadership and discipline spelled doom for almost half their number.

The trail they followed on the 12th ran along the top of a gorge some fifty feet deep through which ran the Truckee River. Along this they carelessly rode some 14 miles, possibly under the observation of Winnemucca's scouts all the way. About two miles from the southern end of Pyramid Lake the mountains on the east closely approached the river. Here the trail dropped down to a narrow bench or strip of bottom land covered with sagebrush. Further on was a grove of cottonwoods.

Some distance beyond these the advance encountered a group of twenty or twenty-five warriors upon a low mound. Beyond this point, around a bend in the river and not in view, were Pah Ute camps. When the volunteers approached they were greeted with a shower of arrows. Realizing they were in a dangerous situation they turned back and made for the cottonwood grove.

The truth is that without being aware of it the whole expedition had ridden into as perfect a trap as could be devised. They had already passed the main body of warriors who were hidden in the sage brush and among the cottonwoods. Upon reaching the cottonwood grove the retreating band found it filled with Indians who loosed a deadly fire upon them. More Indians erupted from the sagebrush to attack the whole column. The strip of bottom land became an inferno of yelling, battle maddened savages and panic stricken white men. But one thought gripped the volunteers' minds. Get back to the place where the trail dropped down from the top of the bluffs. Numaga made one final, despairing effort to restrain his people from what he knew was a fatal error. He threw himself between the warriors and white men in an attempt to obtain a parley. But the Indians, now lusting for blood, disregarded him.

Major Ormsby took command, but could do little. Early in the fight he was shot in the mouth by a poisoned arrow and wounded in both arms. His horse was shot from under him. When the Indians approached, he offered them his revolver as a token of surrender. Disregarding this gesture they killed him. Throughout the battle Bartholomew Riley was conspicuous for cool bravery and unerring marksmanship. Again and again he attempted to rally his comrades for a stand, but it was no use.

The retreat along the narrow bench became a rout as the men crowded upon each other in their efforts to escape while the Indians rode among them hewing them down almost at will. At last the survivors reached the place where the trail mounted upward. Behind them lay the bodies of twenty-six of their comrades. The Indians followed them out upon high ground and killed twenty more.

Later, the Indians said, "White men all cry a heap; got no gun, throw 'um away; got no revolver, throw 'um away too; no want to fight any more now; all big scare, just like cattle, run, run, cry, cry, heap cry, same as papoose; no want Injun to kill 'um any more."

The battle of Pyramid Lake was one of the most tragic disasters in the history of the American frontier. News of it reached Buckland's Station on May 15 when a party of weary survivors among whom was Bartholomew Riley, arrived there. When Riley learned that the Pony Express rider who was due to leave for Smith's Creek, some 90 miles to the east, refused to go, he volunteered to take his place. He made a successful trip in good time. Next day he was mortally wounded by the accidental discharge of a gun in the hands of a friend and died on May 30.

When news of the disaster reached the towns in the Carson River Valley the people were thrown into a panic. The women and children at Virginia City were placed in an unfinished stone house which was fortified to withstand a siege. At Carson City the Penrod Hotel was turned into a fort. The people at Silver City hastily constructed fortifications among rocks on a nearby hill-side and planted imitation cannon to awe the Indians. At Genoa the stone house belonging to Warren Wasson, assistant Indian Agent, was taken over as a refuge. Wasson himself set out for Honey Lake carrying a telegram from General N. S. Clarke, commandant at San Francisco, to the colonel of a cavalry regiment supposed to be stationed there. Governor Roop notified the California authorities of what had happened and asked for help.

The first Pony Express rider going east after the attack upon Williams Station was "Pony Bob" Haslam, who set out for Friday's Station on May 9. If he was not aware of the outbreak when he started, he quickly learned about it when he arrived in Carson City. Since the volunteers had taken all the horses to chase the Pah Utes, there was no change for him. Scores of men were frantically at work fortifying Penrod Hotel and everybody was armed. After feeding his own mount he rode on to Buckland's, 75 miles away. When he arrived he found W. C. Marley, the station keeper, and Johnson Richardson, the rider who was to relieve him, in something of a panic.

Richardson refused to take the *mochila* on and Marley offered Haslam $50 to continue with it. This he agreed to do not because of the bonus, but because he felt it was his duty to do so. Changing horses he pounded on to Sand Springs where he changed again. Making still another change at Cold Spring he arrived safely at Smith's Creek, having covered 190 miles without a rest.

Jay G. Kelley took the *mochila* and raced eastward with the news of the tragedy at William's Station. He made his regular changes along the way, briefly told his story, and pushed on to Ruby Valley, his home station. From there both *mochila* and news were rushed eastward. Every rider along the route, knowing the necessity for both reaching Salt Lake City at the earliest possible moment, outdid himself in an effort to make the best possible time.

Eight hours after arriving at Smith's Creek, Haslam turned back with the west bound *mochila*, possibly on May 12, the day of the battle at Pyramid Lake. At Cold Spring he found that the station

One of the earliest known drawings of the Pony Express. This artist, whose name is unknown, conceived the rider dressed like a jockey on the race track.

had been burnt, the station keeper killed, and the horses driven off. After watering and feeding his own horse, he rode on. Upon reaching Sand Springs he found only the stock tender there whom he persuaded to accompany him for fear he would be killed if left alone.

At Carson Sink he found fifteen men, probably the most of them survivors of the battle at Pyramid Lake, barricaded in the station. Leaving them to hold the place he rode on to Buckland's, arriving only three and a half hours late.

Marley was so overjoyed to see him back alive that he doubled the bonus promised him. After resting an hour and a half he sped on to Carson City, which he found a city of mourning for those slain at Pyramid Lake. He reported to Bolivar Roberts, then rode on to Friday's Station. When he arrived he had covered 380 miles and had been in the saddle thirty-six hours.

The appeal of the people of Carson Valley and Governor Roop met with a ready generous response. Within thirty-six hours after receiving the news of the tragedy at Pyramid Lake, Downieville sent one hundred sixty-five men who arrived at Virginia City after a five days march on foot. Sacramento, Placerville, La Porte,

San Juan, and Nevada City sent volunteers. San Francisco raised money, while General Clarke ordered Captain Stewart of the 3rd Artillery and Captain Flint of the 6th Infantry, one hundred fifty men all told, to march at once to Carson City. That city supplied the largest single group under Colonel John C. Hayes. By the latter part of May about eight hundred men were under arms, two hundred of whom were regular United States soldiers.

On May 26 the combined force took to the field and marched off toward Pyramid Lake to engage the Pah Utes. It was understood that if this could not be done the volunteers were to be disbanded in ten days. The Indians, bloated with pride over their victory on the 12th, were waiting for the army at Big Meadows not far from Williams Station. A skirmish occurred there, in which two white men and six Indians were killed. Winnemucca drew his forces back northward toward Pyramid Lake with the volunteers treading upon his heels. Upon approaching the fatal battleground of the 12th, they found the bodies of the twenty men who had been killed along the trail.

On the afternoon of June 3 a reconnaissance unit advanced close enough to the battle ground itself to count the bodies of twenty-six victims before being driven back. The Indians took a position upon a rocky ledge and defied the white men.

In an attack which lasted three hours the volunteers dislodged them. During the pursuit which followed, twenty-five Indians were killed, fifty horses captured, and the main body driven northward. At sundown the army halted and spent the night in a fortified place called "Fort Storey." Next morning it marched off again, but was unable to contact the Indians. That night earthworks were thrown up and given the name "Fort Haven."

Here the pursuit was abandoned. Colonel Hayes marched his men back to Carson City, where they were disbanded and sent home. Captain Stewart occupied Fort Haven until the middle of July when he moved to Buckland's Station and established Fort Churchill. Indian Agent Frederick Dodge laid out reservations at Pyramid and Walker Lakes and Warren Wasson, with the help of friendly Pah Ute chiefs Young Winnemucca, Oderkoo and

Robert ("Pony Bob") Haslam

Truckee successfully labored to quiet the situation.

Although full scale war was averted, hostile feeling on the part of many of the Pah Utes and raids by small parties continued. The Pony Express was disrupted for about thirty days and harrassed for many months by these predatory bands.

When the news of the outbreak of trouble reached Salt Lake City, request was made of Colonel P. St. George Cooke, commandant at Camp Floyd, for soldiers to be stationed between Sand Springs and Dry Creek. Two companies, ninety men all told, with ten wagons, were ordered out along the Pony Express line to protect emigrants. Howard Egan raised a party of volunteers, made up a wagon train, and left Salt Lake City on June 6, carrying accumulated *mochilas*.

Apparently "Pony Bob" Haslam's epic ride from Friday's

Station to Smith's Creek and back was the last one over Bolivar Roberts' Division. On May 31, C. H. Ruffin, a Pony Express employee, wrote William W. Finney in San Francisco that he and others had been driven out of Cold Creek Station by an Indian attack on the night of May 29. He also said that the men at Dry Creek had been killed and it was thought that the Roberts Creek Station had been destroyed. Both of these reports were correct. William Hamilton, first Pony Express rider out of Sacramento, was at Carson Sink with a number of men and horses and would reach Buckland's on June 1.

At Carson City Bolivar Roberts busied himself with plans for getting his Division back into operation as soon as possible. William W. Finney, hurrying over from San Francisco to help him, made an appeal to the people of Sacramento on June 6 for assistance in getting the job done:

"Will the people of Sacramento help the Pony in its difficulty?" he wrote. "We have conferred some benefits, have asked but little, and perhaps the people will assist. Can anything be done in your city towards paying expenses to furnish arms and provisions for twenty-five men to go through with me to Salt Lake to take and bring on the Express?

"I will be responsible for the return of the arms, will have transportation of my own, and can get men here. What is wanted is $1,000 for the pay of the men, $500 for provisions, and twenty-five Sharp's rifles and as many dragoon pistols. I will guarantee to keep the Pony alive a while longer."

In response to this appeal the people of Sacramento immediately raised the $1500 and most of the arms requested.

By June 9 the party, composed mostly of Pony Express riders, station keepers, and stock tenders, was made up. On that date Bolivar Roberts set out eastward to rebuild destroyed stations and restock them all. This time the buildings were better constructed and five men left to occupy each one until the Indian troubles were over. On June 16 they met Howard Egan at Roberts Creek.

With Egan on his westward journey was William H. Streeper, one of the carriers of the 'heavy mail," whose run was from Diamond Spring to Smith's Creek. One day early in June, before

the Roberts party set out eastward, he saddled his riding mule
"Muggins," loaded his pack mules as usual, and set out westward.
He knew about the trouble with Indians but believed he could
make it safely to Smith's Creek. Moreover, a westward bound
wagon train of emigrants had passed Diamond Spring the day
before. If they could get through, he could. Besides, if it got
dangerous he could travel with them. Some distance east of
Dry Creek he passed them and pushed on ahead. Upon reaching
the station Si McCandless, a "squaw-man" with a Pah Ute wife,
who ran a small trading post across the road, warned him that
he had better keep his eyes open. He suspected that some of his
wife's relatives and friends who had been hanging about the place
for some time were hatching mischief.

When Streeper reached Simpson's Park he found the station
burned, the stock gone, and the keeper, James Alcott dead.
Hurrying on he met the east bound mule mail carrier who upon‑
learning what had happened at Simpson's Park, refused to go any
further. Instead, he turned back with Streeper to Smith's Creek.

The following morning, when Streeper was ready to return,
two prospectors traveling toward Salt Lake City, asked him if
they could accompany him, to which he replied that they could
if they were not afraid of Indians. They fared forth and saw no
Indians or anything else out of the ordinary until they neared
Dry Creek station. They saw no signs of anyone about and a herd
of cattle was moving away from it.

Riding on in Streeper dismounted, walked to the door of the
station and looked inside. Years later he said that what he saw
caused his hair to stand on end. Before him lay the scalped,
mutilated body of Ralph Rosier, the station keeper. John Apple‑
gate and Lafayette ("Bolly") Bolwinkle were not there. Later,
he learned what had happened.

A day or so before, after he had passed on his westward way,
Rosier and Applegate rose early as usual to begin the days work.
"Bolly" was enjoying an extra forty winks before joining them.
Applegate started to make a fire to get breakfast while Rosier
went to the spring for a bucket of water.

Suddenly a rifle shot rang out and Rosier screamed. Applegate leaped to the door, looked out, saw his friend upon the ground dying, and turned back. Another shot, and Applegate fell to the floor, a horrible wound in his hip and groin. A moment later McCandless who was alone in his trading post, dashed across the road and took refuge in the station.

"Bolly" leaped from his bed in his stocking feet, and seized his gun. For some minutes he and McCandless worked like beaver piling grain bags in the doorway and making other preparations to defend the place to the last ditch. Applegate, who was suffering intensely, urged them to abandon him to his fate and attempt to reach the next station. When they refused he asked for a revolver. They gave him one, thinking he wished to take a shot at an Indian. Instead he shot himself through the head.

After the first two shots the attackers seem to have remained quiet, for nothing is said about "Bolly" and McCandless having fought them. At length the trader declared they had to make a run of it to the next station. When "Bolly" objected on the grounds that the Indians would certainly cut them down in the open, McCandless assured him such was not the case. They were not after him, he said, and since he had always treated them well they had a friendly feeling for him. If 'Bolly" would stay close to him they would not dare shoot for fear of hitting him.

"Bolly" at length agreed to make the attempt. When everything was ready, the grain bags were removed from the door and they leaped outside. As they dashed down the road McCandless kept between "Bolly" and the Indians. A few gave chase on foot, but the fugitives outdistanced them. Being satisfied with the blood they had already shed, they turned back to loot the station.

"Bolly" and McCandless reached the next station in safety where they found three or four men ready to defend it. Having covered the ten or twelve miles without boots "Bolly's" feet were so cut by stones and filled with cactus thorns that he was laid up for some time.

Early in June Elijah N. Wilson set out from Schell Creek to make his regular run to Deep Creek. When he reached his destination he found that the rider who was to take the *mochila* on was not there. Pushing on to Willow Spring he learned that the man had been killed on his run. Since his horse was worn out he had to stop and let him rest a while.

About four o'clock in the afternoon seven Indians rode in to demand that Peter Neece, the station keeper, give them something to eat. Neece offered them a twenty-four pound sack of flour, which was indignantly refused. They wanted a sack each instead. At that he tossed the flour back into the station and ordered them to clear out. He would give them nothing. This so angered them that as they passed the corral they filled an old, lame cow with arrows. Seeing this act of wanton cruelty Neece drew his revolver and killed two of them.

Knowing that about thirty of them were camped not far off, and that an attack would almost certainly be made, they loaded all the empty guns they had and prepared to defend themselves. Just before dark they saw a cloud of dust in the distance which advertised the fact that the Indians were coming. Adopting the strategy of lying down upon the ground in the sagebrush they waited.

Soon the Indians arrived and were greeted by gunfire from outside the station. This so confused them that they milled about in more or less confusion. Some of them attempted to return the fire by aiming at the gun flashes. This however, was not effective, for each time one of the defenders fired he instantly leaped to one side. Many years later Wilson said that although he had two revolvers he did little except jump from spot to spot. Finally he landed in a small ravine where he remained until the Indians rode off in disgust. When he joined his companions they praised him for his part in the affair but he would have none of it. Credit for the victory, he said, belonged entirely to them.

On the night of July 3 William F. Fisher and George W. ("Wash") Perkins set out eastward from Ruby Valley. They kept a sharp lookout and avoided those spots where an Indian ambush might be expected. At one of these points, however, there was no detour around the point of possible danger. Putting spurs to their horses they dashed through it. Indians were waiting for them, and before they reached safety a bullet went through Fisher's hat and an arrow lodged in Perkins' *mochila*. Perkins remained at Simpson's Spring while Fisher rode on alone to Salt Lake City. When he arrived he had used six horses and two mules. The distance he had covered on this ride was 300 miles.

In September Elijah N. Wilson was sent along the line from Schell Creek to Antelope station with a number of horses. He made the trip safely, delivered his charges, and started back the next day. When he reached Spring Valley station he found two young men who invited him to stay for dinner.

Wilson accepted the invitation and turned his horse loose, thinking it would go to the stable in the corral. Instead it joined some others which were grazing behind the station. A short time later they saw Indians driving all of the horses across a meadow toward a cedar grove a short distance away. They ran after the thieves on foot, but the animals entered the trees before they could be overtaken.

As he ran, Wilson fired his revolver, but without effect. Having outdistanced his companions he entered the cedars ahead of them. As he ran around a large one, an arrow struck him in the forehead about two inches above the left eye and lodged there. He fell to the ground unconscious. The young men came up and did what they could for him. When they tried to pull the arrow out the shaft came loose leaving the point stuck in his forehead. The Indians got away with all the horses.

Being certain Wilson would die the young men rolled him into the shade of the cedar and set out for the next station on foot. On the following day they came back with some men to bury him. Finding him still alive they carried him into the station and a messenger was sent to Ruby Valley, a full days ride each way, for a doctor. Upon his arrival he removed the arrow point, but there was little else he could do. He told the young men to keep a wet rag on the wound and went back. For six days Wilson lay fighting for his life with only such rude nursing as his friends could give him.

No doubt he would have died had not Howard Egan come along, possibly on his way back to Salt Lake City. The Division Superintendent took one look at him, then sent a rider post haste to Ruby Valley to bring the doctor back. For twelve days longer Wilson lay in a stupor, hovering between life and death. Then to everyone's delight he began to mend. In a short time he was able to ride again. The wound left such an unsightly scar upon his forehead that ever after he wore his hat outdoors and indoors to hide it.

In the early part of October a war party of eighty Pah Utes descended upon Egan's station while Mike Holt station keeper, and a rider by the name of Wilson were at breakfast. Leaping to their feet they grabbed their guns and began firing upon them. The Indians had no guns, but filled with confidence of victory due to overwhelming numbers, they swooped in for the kill. Holton and Wilson fought heroically and kept them at bay until their ammunition was exhausted. Then, as the Indians broke through the door they heard the chief utter the one word "bread."

Hoping to satisfy them, and thus escape death, the white men piled all the bread in the station on the table. To their dismay the chief remained unsatisfied. Pointing to the sacks of flour piled in one corner he ordered them to build a fire and bake more. Throughout the day Holton and Wilson continued to supply bread to their ravenous, unwelcome guests. As they worked they talked about William Dennis, rider from the west who was due to arrive late in the afternoon. When he did not come they concluded the Indians had killed him.

About sundown, the stock of flour having been exhausted, the chief ordered Holton and Wilson taken outside and tied to a wagon tongue which had been driven into the ground. Having done this they proceeded to pile sage brush at their feet with the expectation of roasting them alive. Then, they set it afire and began to dance and yell like demons.

But the Indians had not gotten Dennis. As he approached the station he saw the savages from the distance, whirled his horse around, and raced back the way he had come. They were so

"Swimming the Storm Swollen Stream" from *Hutchings California Magazine*, July 1860. Earliest drawing of Pony Express rider.

busy celebrating the torture of Holton and Wilson they did not see him. About five miles back he had passed Lieutenant Weed and sixty United States dragoons on their way east to Salt Lake City. Upon being informed of what was going on at the station they swept ahead full tilt, roared down upon the scene, and caught the merrymaking savages by surprise in time to prevent injury to the captives. When it was over the Indians had lost eighteen warriors and sixty horses.

The regular schedule for the Pony Express was resumed on July 7, but raids by small parties of young warriors anxious to make a reputation for themselves continued for a year or so. Bancroft said the company lost 150 horses, seven stations, and sixteen men killed. The rebuilding of stations, pay to increased personnel, raise in wages, and other expenses amounted to about $75,000. This was a heavy blow for a company that was already bankrupt and going deeper into debt even under the most favorable of circumstances.

Newspapers and the public highly praised the Central Overland California & Pike's Peak Express Company for the manner in which it met the crisis but that, pleasant though it was, did not pay bills or liquidate deficits. Being a private enterprise the government was totally oblivious to its needs. The fact that it was rendering a vital service to the troubled nation by maintaining rapid communication with California was not taken into account.

Critics still insisted that the Pony would have to quit running when winter brought on severe cold, bad roads, and snow. But it didn't. A new schedule, which allowed eleven days between telegraph terminals and fifteen from St. Joseph to Sacramento was set up. On November 24 the *Sacramento Union* remarked that the Pony continued his "usual gallop" and that notwithstanding winter weather over a quarter of the route and snow three inches deep he made it from Salt Lake City to that town in three days and twenty minutes.

10

THE FATEFUL YEAR, 1860

VIEWED FROM THE ANGLE of efficiency, the Pony Express was all that its promoters promised and much more than most people expected of it. Aside from the short period of the Pah Ute War, when it was temporarily halted, it ran on schedule and made deliveries with amazing regularity. Even during that period the mail was only delayed, for as already mentioned, Bolivar Roberts at Carson City and Howard Egan at Salt Lake City enlisted volunteers and carried the *mochilas* through.

When difficulties and distance are taken into consideration, no better job was ever done in the history of the United States mail service. The men who planned and supervised it, and the youths who rode the lonely route day and night, in fair weather and foul, in peace or in war, deserve the highest praise.

The whole organization from the home office in St. Joseph to the loneliest station on the Utah or Nevada desert was as well articulated as a military unit. To the dismay of critics and delight of friends it worked beautifully. Even the annoying Pah Ute War was not without its advantages, for it served as a means of publicizing the heroic achievements of the fearless riders.

Although the amount of mail carried by the Pony Express was far less than was anticipated, its speed in delivery served as an occasion for increased complaints against Butterfield's "Ox-Bow" route. With the Civil War on the horizon the people in California and newspapers in the East fumed against the time required by both it and the sea route via Panama. The Pony Express proved that letters and important dispatches could be delivered in ten or twelve days and the westerners wanted no more mail by either route.

In the end, and under normal circumstances, there probably would have been readjustments, compromises, reorganizations, and the establishment of lines to the reasonable satisfaction of everyone. But circumstances were not normal in a number of important respects. In fact, the whole picture presents an interesting study of success, failure, insoluble financial problems, brilliant administration, the sordid clash of estimable personalities, and the distant, yet unmistakable rumblings of civil war.

The Pah Ute War of midsummer, 1860, was not the only difficulty confronting the Central Overland California & Pikes Peak Express Company. There were quarrels among the top-flight executives which shook the company to its very foundations and seriously handicapped its operations. For months distrust and criticism of Robert B. Bradford's judgement and management of R. B. Bradford & Company in Denver, and even of his character, had been growing in the minds of his partners, especially in those of Russell and Waddell.

They complained about the small amount of gold he forwarded to Leavenworth, protested against his building of houses,

Courtesy of Charles R. Mabey

From *The Pony Express* by Charles R. Mabey.

laying out of new towns, and the buying of stock in toll roads, irrigation projects, coal mines, and ranches. They said all this indicated a neglect of company business and even lent an ear to the report that he was carrying on with a young school teacher he had imported from the East.

Bradford, in numerous letters to Waddell, vigorously defended himself, while Russell, who ignored Bradford's letters to him, wrote bitterly to Waddell. Majors, with characteristic calm detachment, and because he knew more about the gold region from having visited it than did Russell and Waddell, sat upon the sidelines. Bradford journeyed back to Lexington in September 1860, talked matters over with Waddell, but the criticism continued.

There were also quarrels among the top flight executives of the Central Overland California & Pike's Peak Express Company which shook it to the very foundations and seriously handicapped its efforts. From the very beginning William H. Russell and Benjamin F. Ficklin disagreed sharply on policies of management. To the latter was committed considerable authority as Route Superintendent in the actual operation of the Pony Express and stage coach lines.

Circumstances being what they were, with Russell in Washington and New York, Waddell tied in Leavenworth and Lexington, and Alexander Majors supervising the Russell, Majors & Waddell wagon trains on the road, Ficklin became in reality the operational head of the company. This did not disturb Majors, Waddell, or Jones, who were upon the ground and in daily contact with affairs, but it did Russell. He felt he was being by-passed, as perhaps he was to some degree. Having been the acknowledged chief executive for so long, he hotly resented any authority being delegated to Ficklin or anybody else. The result was an irreconcilable quarrel between the two.

The first that is known of Ficklin in the West is as a member of William M. F. McGraw's surveying party of one hundred men in 1857, whose business it was to lay out the United States Overland Wagon road from South Pass to Salt Lake City. When that work was halted by Mormon difficulties and the appearance of United States troops in Utah, McGraw turned his equipment over to General A. S. Johnston and released his men. Since winter was already upon them, fifty or sixty of them enlisted in the army and the others returned home to the Missouri River. Ficklin was appointed Deputy United States Marshal, served for several months as such, then entered the service of General Johnston.

Hard service, lack of grass, and the capture of horses and mules by the Mormons had all but reduced Johnston's army to infantry. Replacements had to be found before spring. Captain R. B. Marcy was sent south on a midwinter journey to Taos, New Mexico, and Ficklin off to the north to Beaverhead Valley on the Jefferson Fork of the Missouri River to buy them. This place was a favorite winter haven for trappers and mountain men. He left Camp Scott at Fort Bridger December 9 with ten men, twelve horses, six pack mules, and thirty days rations. They had no guide and no knowledge of the trail. The snow on the mountains was two feet deep, and in many places the men had to break trail for the animals.

In order to avoid a Mormon settlement, said to have been established on Snake River near the mouth of Blackfoot Creek, he struck out upon a new, unknown route to the divide between that river and the Missouri River. A storm came on, and they had to make a forced march of thirty miles to reach lower altitude. Their provisions gave out, they were compelled to kill some of their animals for food, and suffering from the cold was intense.

When they reached Beaverhead Valley they found nobody there. The mountain men, fearful of raids by Mormons, had moved to Clark's Fork of the Missouri River. Ficklin followed them and made contracts for beef cattle and horses to be delivered at Camp Scott.

The party returned on January 20, after suffering much hardship. They had encountered from three to six feet of snow, many of them were disabled by snow blindness and all of them were more or less frost bitten. Early in April Ficklin set out for the East with dispatches.

Late in 1859 he succeeded Beverley D. Williams as Route Superintendent for the Leavenworth & Pike's Peak Express Company. The job he did cleaning up the line, with the help of Joseph A. Slade, so won the admiration and approval of his employers that when the Central Overland California & Pike's Peak Express Company was formed he was admitted as one of the incorporators and assigned to the same job.

He held no stock in the company, was merely an employee, and his responsibility was to see that the Pony Express and stage coaches ran on schedule. Naturally, he enjoyed wide discretion and authority in the discharge of it. It could not have been otherwise. Without a doubt much of the credit for putting the Pony Express into operation in sixty-five days was due to his energy and ability.

By midsummer of 1860 Russell had become violently opposed to him and wholly dissatisfied with his work. Matters came to a head while the Pah Ute War was going on and on June 6 Ficklin wired Russell his resignation. As a postscript he added, "Send a man to take my place damned quick." This "profane, insulting dispatch," as Russell called it, stirred him to action. On the 12th he telegraphed Waddell and Jones instruction to call a meeting of the Executive Committee of the company and accept the resignation.

Waddell and Jones refused to do this because they felt Ficklin was a valuable man and should be retained. This so angered Russell that he tendered his own resignation as president of the company and offered Majors and Waddell his stock in it for $500,000. They did not take him up on either proposition.

Russell said that Ficklin had been treated too well, given too much authority, was self-willed, not subject to instructions, inclined to rule or ruin, was working up a big name for himself, and knew nothing about economy. Instead of accepting Russell's resignation Waddell and Jones wrote him a conciliatory telegram and Ficklin wrote an apology. It was all in vain however, for as Russell said, his determination not to work with Ficklin any longer was as fixed as the "law of the Medes and Persians."

Ficklin quit, Russell was mollified, but Majors, Waddell, and Jones still felt they had lost a good man. The ousted Route Superintendent went to Washington where he submitted a bid to the Post Office Department for a mail contract which would have provided him with a Pony Express of his own. Evidently his quarrel with Russell and the loss of his job did him no damage, for Hiram Sibley and Jeptha H. Wade took him into the new Pacific Telegraph Company as an incorporator.

When the Civil War broke out he hurried to Virginia. On April 25, 1861, he was commissioned major by Governor John Letcher of that state and assigned to the Virginia Volunteers, Department of Transportation. It is said that he was very successful in supplying the Confederate Army with goods in spite of blockades. After the war he engaged in establishing stage lines in southwestern states and Indian Territory in cooperation with General Armstrong. He became wealthy, was well known to stage men of that region, and died in Washington at Willard's Hotel by choking on a fish bone.

Overshadowing all other problems and difficulties confronting the Central Overland California & Pike's Peak Express Company in 1860 was that of finances. As early as January of that year its bank accounts were overdrawn and heavy obligations overdue. Not long after the Pony Express went into operation Russell asked that his stock in the company be sent him. He hoped to borrow $50,000 on it and advised Majors and Waddell to use theirs for the same purpose.

Russell complained that his partners were not raising enough money in the West and flatly said they were compelling him to bear the major portion of the financial burden. Waddell retorted that Russell was neglecting the business in the West and spending too much money in the East promoting it. He also severely criticised the policy of maintaining offices in Chicago and New York.

The truth of the matter was, Waddell saw the handwriting on the wall and was frightened by it. Russell also saw it, would not admit it, and with characteristic sanguinity hoped to avoid the doom it proclaimed. He spoke of financial difficulties confronting him and of fascinating prospects of better days in the same letter. Always he saw a way out.

By the middle of June, 1860, Waddell's criticisms became so stringent that Russell was ready to quit:

"I cannot longer represent the Express Company in any shape," he wrote. "If after all my toil and sacrifice I am to be *really* abused for my course, it is high time that some other and more competent man be placed at the head of it. Hope the appointment of an agent to represent the company will be telegraphed today or tomorrow . . . I hope to close a mail contract for the company today or tomorrow. Will do so if I can. Then I am done . . . My stock is for sale, first to the company, as agreed upon, next to you and Mr. Majors, and if neither of you want it then to any outsider who will pay you cash or secure you to your satisfaction . . . at a valuation of $500,000."

This so frightened Waddell that he hurriedly wrote an apology which restored peace, but not harmony. The quarrel had cut too deep for that. With greatly relieved feelings Russell attacked the knotty problem of meeting obligations and carrying on the business.

The plain fact is that the firm of Russell, Majors & Waddell had been bankrupt since the winter of 1857-58. Since it constituted what might be called a sort of holding company for R. B. Bradford & Company, the Leavenworth & Pike's Peak Express Company, and the Central Overland California & Pike's Peak Express Company they all labored under the shadow of insolvency. The cause was the so called Mormon War in Utah.

In May, 1857, while Russell, Majors & Waddell wagons were being loaded to transport military supplies to posts in the west and southwest, the Administration in Washington ordered a small army of 2,500 men to concentrate at Fort Leavenworth, march to Utah under General W. S. Harney, and bring Brigham Young, and his recalcitrant Mormons into line. Before it reached its destination, Harney was removed from command and General A. S. Johnston appointed in his stead.

On June 19, a month or so after the last Russell, Majors & Waddell wagon took to the road, Captain Thomas L. Brent, Quartermaster at Fort Leavenworth informed Russell that his firm would be required to transport some 3,000,000 pounds of supplies for Johnston's army.

Russell was dismayed at this, for the season for starting on a long haul of that kind was past. Moreover the firm's entire equipment was already upon the road elsewhere. To comply with that order meant buying about 1,000 wagons and equipment for them, from 8 to 10,000 oxen, and the employment of 1,200 to 1,500 men. All of this represented an investment of $500,000 or more.

After all, he couldn't refuse because he had enjoyed a monopoly on the freighting of military supplies since 1855. He threw his great organization into high gear with the result that between the middle of July and first of August 1,000 wagons, enough to make up forty trains carrying 4,525,913 pounds of supplies left Fort Leavenworth with the army. Already, far to the west, the snow was beginning to fall upon the Rocky Mountains through which they must pass. Just as the lead trains were clearing South Pass late in August they were ordered to halt on Green River, Ham's Fork, and Black's Fork.

Brigham Young got word of the plan before the advance units left Fort Leavenworth. On September 15 he declared martial law in Utah, forbade United States troops to enter the Territory, ordered out his militia, and instructed them to stampede stock, block roads, burn grass, destroy fords, and harass the army in every possible way, but shed no blood.

This order was obeyed to the letter. On the night of October 4, Russell, Majors & Waddell's trains 21 and 25 under wagon masters John M. Dawson and R. W. Barrett were captured by Major Lot Smith on Green River. The same night, train 26 under wagonmaster Lewis Simpson was seized by Porter Rockwell on Big Sandy Creek. The oxen were all driven off and the wagons, which contained 300,000 pounds of provisions, enough to last the whole army three months, were burned. This loss to the contractors was later written down at $72,000.

On November 2 General A. S. Johnston ordered the army to abandon the march toward Salt Lake City, proceed to Fort Bridger, and set up winter quarters. About noon of the day the march began, a heavy snow storm descended. What grass the Mormons had not burned was soon covered by seven inches of snow. That night raiding Saints drove off 500 more oxen, 150 of which belonged to Russell, Majors & Waddell.

On the night of the 7th more than half the remaining oxen died of overwork, starvation, and cold. The advance reached Fort Bridger on the 16th or 17th, having consumed ten days marching 35 miles. Since the Mormons had burned the Fort some time before, there were no buildings available for storing supplies. Therefore, as Russell, Majors & Waddell wagons were unloaded, the boxes were broken up to build sheds.

James Rupe, General Agent for Russell, Majors & Waddell, and Charles Morehead, his assistant, made up an inventory of losses sustained on the march and made a mid-winter journey back across the frigid plains to Fort Leavenworth with it. When they wired Russell a resume of it, he ordered them to come on to Washington.

In the spring of 1858 a bill for losses sustained on that march was made up and presented to the government. It totaled $493,-553.01, not a dime of which was ever paid. In other words, practically the entire amount invested in equipment to transport supplies to Utah was a total loss.

When Russell presented the bills of lading Rupe and Morehead had carried across the plains, which constituted evidence of service rendered to the War Department, he was told there was no money with which to pay them. The Department had exceeded its appropriation and nothing could be done without a special act of Congress.

To further complicate matters it was announced on January 11, 1858, that 3,018 officers and men would be sent to Utah that year to reinforce General Johnston. A few days later the firm signed a two-year contract based upon the transportation of 10,000,000 pounds of supplies to posts in the west, southwest, and Utah. That was more than double the amount transported in 1857. Since most of the forty trains sent to Utah in 1857 had been lost, the expenditure for new outfits to carry on the business in 1858 would be enormous.

With the help of the War and Quartermaster's Departments and powerful friends in Congress, a Deficiency Bill to relieve the former was put through the House. Debate upon it, however, opened the whole question of the "Utah War." Both Houses called for copies of all contracts for transporting supplies, the Administration was savagely attacked, and Russell, Majors & Waddell held up to public scorn as "chiseling contractors." The Bill was passed, but the firm had been so besmirched that its credit was seriously impaired.

Not long after the 1858-60 contract was signed, Russell laid the bald facts concerning his firm's financial status before Secretary of War, John B. Floyd. Since the War Department had no funds with which to pay its bills, and the firm had none with which to equip itself for the huge task confronting it, he suggested that he be allowed to draw acceptances upon the Department in anticipation of its earnings for 1858. In brief, he proposed to collect pay for transportation that year in advance.

It was understood that the Secretary would endorse them, none of them would ever be presented to the War Department for payment, and Russell, Majors & Waddell would retire them as they fell due. Incidentally, when the fact that they were being issued in large amounts was brought to the attention of Attorney General Bates, he promptly declared them illegal on the ground that Secretary Floyd had no authority to do so. Later, the United States Court of Claims upheld his opinion.

Having agreed to the plan, Secretary Floyd wrote letters to bankers and financiers urging them to lend Russell large sums of money upon the acceptances as security. Among these were August Belmont, the Bank of America, the Bank of the Republic in New York, Riggs & Company, and Kilgore, Wilson & Company of Washington, and a number of individuals. Russell's problem for 1858 was solved, but he solved it by mortgaging the future and multiplied difficulties in days to come. He sowed to the wind and reaped the whirlwind.

The total amount of acceptances issued from March 25, 1858 to October 13, 1860, was $5,036,127.50. Some of these were retired outright from time to time and others by new ones issued to replace them. John Perry Sellar, clerk of the Trustees of Russell, Majors & Waddell reported in 1862 that there were outstanding $861,000 of these to which should be added the $870,000 involved in the bond transaction in Washington as will be shown later. Russell, Majors & Waddell's total indebtedness represented by the acceptances alone was $1,731,000.

To further complicate Russell's financial problems, in 1860 there was delay in ordering out supplies for the military posts in the West. Russell, Majors & Waddell assumed that the trains would leave at the usual time and got ready for it. Wagons, oxen, and equipment were bought on credit, and large numbers of men employed.

Since they were paid only upon the presentation of bills of lading showing delivery of supplies to their destination, the receipt of sorely needed pay for transportation was postponed week after week. Meanwhile notes for thirty, sixty, and one hundred twenty days, given in the purchase of equipment and loans falling due in midsummer went to protest. Day by day the firm's credit sagged to lower levels. The bulk of the supplies were ordered out in August and September, four to five months late, but much damage had already been done.

Meanwhile the old, irritating question of an overland mail was being considered in Congress. After various plans had been presented and discussed without results, a group of men, among them Russell no doubt, got up a bill and gave it to Senator Hale to introduce. It provided for a tri-weekly mail over the Central Route at $600,000 for the first year and daily thereafter not to exceed $200,000 additional. The usual sectional lines were drawn, Senator William M. Gwin of California presented one of his own, and the matter dragged on for several months.

Russell vigorously threw himself into the controversy. He lined up available influence, which was considerable, and strengthened his connections with the Post Office Department. On June 13 he wrote Waddell that he expected to close a contract for an overland mail, not the one proposed in Hale's bill, which would pay $600,000 per year. He also said that although it was not as good as they wanted, it would "lay the foundation" for one that would pay $1,200,000.

Seven days before Congress adjourned he wrote Waddell that he did not think that body would pass a bill for mail service on the Central Route. Since it had cut the appropriation for ocean service out of the Post Office bill, he said the Department would be free to contract with the Central Overland California & Pike's Peak Express Company to transport it all at a good price. As he predicted, Congress adjourned without doing anything and Russell's hopes mounted.

The contract he hoped to secure could be made by the Post Office Department without Congressional action as a public necessity. After that body adjourned, Senator Gwin wrote President Buchanan saying he had been induced to believe by conversations with him and the Postmaster General that if public necessity demanded a contract for carrying letters and printed matter over the Central Route, one would be let. That necessity, he said, had arisen.

In the same letter he stated that Russell, Majors & Waddell had offered to carry it tri-weekly in twenty-five days for the first year for $900,000 and six times a week thereafter for the same compensation. He strongly recommended that their offer be accepted. In this he was probably attempting to fulfill a promise of a mail contract over the Central Route made before the Pony Express was started. The Senator's plea was in vain, the Postmaster General made a temporary contract for ocean service, and Russell was left just where he was when Congress convened. Had he gotten this contract, this story would doubtless have a different ending. The reason for his failure was irreconcilable sectional differences in Congress and the Administration.

By mid-July Russell and Waddell both frankly spoke of "going down" in their correspondence. Waddell began to fear it long before, but Russell was tardy in acknowledging the possibility of it. As James Aull said of him twenty-five or thirty years before, he was always sanguine. He believed he would be able to put through something which would solve their problems and the record shows that he was not lacking in plans or energy in attempting to work them out.

Receiving Pony Express mail from train.

The failure to secure the "public necessity" mail contract sealed his doom. By mid-summer, 1860, the situation was well nigh out of control. His paper, including Secretary Floyd's acceptances, was daily going to protest, he had borrowed money from almost everyone he could, and sinister reports concerning his solvency circulated freely.

At this time he met and received from Godard Bailey, clerk in the Department of the Interior and custodian of the "Indian Trust Fund," $150,000 in bonds belonging to that Fund. How and where they met, by whom they were introduced, and what Bailey's motives in the transaction may have been are matters of secondary importance. The only condition Bailey made was that the bonds should be merely used as collateral in securing short term loans and the identical ones be returned to him. Russell said later that he did not inquire into Bailey's right to let him have the securities, was not aware of their real ownership, and assumed he was doing nothing wrong in accepting them. There is no good reason why his statement regarding this transaction should not be accepted as the truth.

Russell took the bonds to New York where he was able to borrow only $97,000 on them, which was insufficient to relieve the pressure upon Russell, Majors & Waddell. Some $300,000 of acceptances were about to go to protest in that city and the picture was darker than ever. Consequently he again met Bailey and told him the stark truth. Bailey also had some stark truth to reveal. He informed Russell that the $150,000 in bonds did not belong to him and he had no right whatever to let him have them. The Department of the Interior was merely custodian for the real owners, certain Indian tribes in the West. Russell instantly saw the grim situation in which he had become involved. To make matters worse some of the bonds had already been sold into the hands of innocent purchasers and others were about to be.

The alternatives confronting him were harsh indeed. He would be exposed, disgraced, and charged with a serious crime if those bonds were not returned. Other acceptances would go to protest and be presented to the War Department for payment, with the result that Secretary Floyd would be ruined unless they were paid. And he had no money to redeem the bonds or liquidate the acceptances.

What he did was get $387,000 more of Indian Trust Fund bonds from Bailey. This time he knew exactly what he was doing and what the consequences would be if exposed. He also knew the ugly name by which such transactions went. Nevertheless he took them. Whether Bailey urged them upon him is beside the point. He also knew that solving his financial difficulties was an extremely doubtful matter, even with this batch of securities.

On September 29, 1860, he wrote Samuel & Allen in St. Louis a long letter in which he said that some $70,000 in acceptances was then under protest. To care for them and meet all future obligations would require $400,000. With the efficient help of that firm he got it. During August and September he received $160,943.84 from the War Department as pay for transportation. Between October 1 and 11 he wrote $150,000 in acceptances upon

Secretary Floyd and from the 11th to the 13th $120,000 more. During August, September, and October his receipts from bonds gotten from Bailey, pay for transportation, funds from Samuel & Allen, and acceptances, even after liberal discounts were allowed on both bonds and acceptances, was in excess of $700,000. This was exclusive of receipts from the Central Overland California & Pike's Peak Express Company and the Pony Express. Huge though the total was, it was insufficient.

While Russell was going deeper into the mire every day in Washington, Alexander Majors accurately read the signs of the times and took measures he knew would have to be taken sooner or later anyway. On October 17 he gave a deed of trust to Alexander W. Street for the benefit of individuals to whom he, Russell, Majors & Waddell, or the Central Overland California & Pike's Peak Express Company were indebted. Liabilities listed amounted to $37,167.56. Among the assets were some 2,000 acres of Jackson County land, town lots in Shawnee and Olathe, Kansas, interest in the West Kansas City Company, slaves, farming implements, etc. Two days later he gave another which listed liabilities of $75,540.74.

The effect of Majors' bankruptcy upon the business and financial structure of the Middle West was like that of an earthquake upon a limited area. For years Russell, Majors & Waddell's paper had circulated freely and was considered a sound medium of exchange. Banks, business houses of all kinds, and individuals took it without question. When news that Majors had made assignments leaked out, hundreds of people who held notes, acceptances, etc. rushed to dispose of them, only to discover they were unable to do so.

In the latter part of November Russell got $333,000 more of Trust Fund bonds from Godard Bailey, making a grand total of $870,000 worth he illegally appropriated to his own use. As a gesture he deposited an equal amount of Secretary Floyd's acceptances and a note upon Russell, Majors & Waddell with Bailey as security.

Russell was through, Lincoln was elected, Southern states were moving to make good their threat to secede if a Republican were seated in the White House, a panic hit Wall Street, securities of all kinds hit the skids, and the holders of the Trust Fund bonds demanded wider margins.

On December 22 Bailey confessed what he had done. Both he and Russell were arrested, the latter in his New York office on Christmas Day, and put into prison. A short time later both were released on bond.

On January 14, 1861, Russell voluntarily appeared before a Select Committee of the House which had been appointed to inquire into both the bond transaction and the matter of Secretary Floyd's acceptances. He again appeared on the 23d and 25th. Since he was under criminal prosecution and could not be compelled to testify he was not questioned very closely. On January 29th he, together with Bailey and Floyd, were indicted by a District of Columbia grand jury, the latter for having illegally endorsed the acceptances. None of them were ever brought to trial.

Neither Russell, Majors & Waddell nor the government reimbursed the holders of the acceptances. In 1863 the United States Court of Claims ruled that they were illegal. Neither did the firm repay the $870,000 worth of Indian Trust Fund bonds Russell got. On July 8, 1862, House Bill No. 554 to reimburse that Fund was presented to the Senate. It was passed and signed by President Lincoln. The total cost to the government, including interest, was $710,458.65, not a dollar of which was recovered from the partner's estates.

Beginning about January 1, 1861, Russell, Majors, and Waddell executed deeds of trust for the benefit of creditors by which they stripped themselves of their possessions. The best index to the amount of their obligations is Russell's Schedule of Indebtedness in his application to the District Court of the United States for the Southern District of New York in 1868, for a decree of bankruptcy. The amount, including the Indian Trust Fund bonds, was $1,662,342.16. This did not include the personal debts of any of them.

Their monopoly on the freighting of military supplies to posts in the west was ended and the firm of Russell, Majors & Waddell was dissolved. The great organization that had once crowded the long, dusty trails with its wagons and oxen passed into oblivion without a successor.

The Central Overland California & Pike's Peak Express Company was all that was left of the vast transportation empire and interrelated partnerships. Being a corporation, Russell, Majors, and Waddell were not individually responsible for its debts. During those cataclysmic days when Russell's world was disintegrating, its stages ran with usual regularity and the Pony Express operated on schedule. It experienced difficulties, however, and its employees, with good reason, dubbed it "Clean Out of Cash & Poor Pay."

11

DEFEAT AND COMPROMISE

RUSSELL stayed on in Washington to salvage
what he could from the wreck of his enterprises
and hopes. In spite of the somber facts concerning the Indian
Trust Fund bonds, he was not lacking in powerful friends and
supporters. Two days after his arrest Thomas P. Akers, Lexing-
tonian, former pastor of the Methodist Episcopal Church there,
member of the 34th Congress, and orator wrote Waddell a long
letter in which he characterized the whole affair as a plot concocted by President Buchanan and his cabinet, especially Secretary Floyd, "to entangle and victimize" Russell and "offer him
up as a victim of popular clamor in order to screen the deformities
of a rotten and falling administration."

This explanation was apparently widely circulated, for H. H.
Bancroft took notice of it in his *Chronicles of the Builders.*

"Russell," he said, "fell into a difficulty, if indeed, it were not a
trap set for him by the friends of the Southern Route . . . He was
induced to take $830,000 in bonds of the Interior Department as
a loan . . ."

Russell himself, in his Statement to the Public as published in
the newspapers of March 28, 1861, fails to utter a single word to
the effect that he was "trapped" by anybody. Neither did he
say anything to that effect before the Select Committee. With
remarkable candor he confessed that he knew what he was doing
when he got the second and third lot of bonds. His only de-
fense for participating in an embezzlement of great magnitude was
that the government owed his firm a large sum of money for
losses in Utah in 1857-58.

During the days immediately following the debacle, Russell's
sanguine nature bounced back to the surface. Whatever discour-
agement or remorse he may have felt over what had happened
was cloaked under an irrepressible attitude of optimism. Although
under almost unbearable strain, and with a criminal indictment

hanging over him, his letters to Waddell were calm, businesslike, and detached.

Although Waddell and Majors viewed the state of affairs as hopeless from the beginning, Russell assured them everything would turn out right in the end. On February 11, 1861, he chided Waddell for being discouraged.

"You talk as though you do not expect to pay through," he wrote. "I do, and feel entire confidence."

In the same letter he expressed satisfaction over a proposed resolution in Congress to appoint a Commission to inquire into the whole affair. There was also talk of the government bringing suit against Russell, Majors & Waddell to recover the value of the bonds, but neither of these things was done. Russell hoped one of them would, for, as he said, the claim for losses in Utah could be brought in. He closed the letter with the characteristic comment,

"Have great faith in getting mail contract all right."

Courtesy of St. Joseph Public Library

Pony Express cover. Front of letter sent on first run out of San Francisco, California. The only known one bearing postmarks of both Sacramento and St. Joseph which was carried on the first run.

The contract he had "great faith" in securing was authorized by the annual Post Route Bill introduced into the Senate on February 2, 1861, which he fully expected would pass. It provided for a daily mail for six days a week with pay of $800,000 per year. The "Battle of the Routes" was joined again, for the Overland Mail Company was a strong contender for the contract. Nevertheless, the proposition of consolidating the Central Overland California & Pike's Peak Express Company and Overland Mail Company lines to California on the Central Route was discussed in the meetings of the Post Office and Post Roads Committee, but nothing came of it at the time.

While the contest was at its height, and the two chambers echoing with oratory, word reached Washington that the Overland Mail Company line had been "cut up by the roots" in Texas by Confederate forces. Plainly, a crisis, about which something had to be done without delay, had arisen. Regular communication with California had to be maintained at any cost. Seven states had already seceded, others were moving in the same direction, and strong pressure was being brought to bear upon California to take the same solemn step.

The problem confronting the administration was a difficult, embarrassing one. The mail to California *had* to go through, but it's favored line, the Southern Route, was closed. That left only one alternative, the Central Route, which was already preempted by the Central Overland California & Pike's Peak Express Company with its contracts to Salt Lake City and Sacramento. With two experienced, competent contractors on its hands, neither of whom could be honorably discharged, some new plan had to be adopted.

There is ample evidence that Russell and William B. Dinsmore, president of the Overland Mail Company, came to an agreement some time about the middle of February, 1861. Because of this the Post Route Bill enjoyed smooth passage through both Houses and was passed on March 2. It provided for the bodily removal of the Overland Mail Company to the Central Route, a daily mail six days a week from the Missouri River to Placerville, California, the operation of a Pony Express twice a week until the completion of the transcontinental telegraph line, with pay of $1,000,000 per year. It was to become effective the following July 1.

On March 16, 1861, Russell and Dinsmore signed a contract on behalf of their respective companies under which the work of carrying the mail over the Central Route to California was divided between them. This contract also covered the express and passenger business and the operation of the Pony Express. Thus the Post Route Bill and the contract signed by Russell and Dinsmore achieved what had been discussed in the Post Office and Post Roads Committee early in the year, the consolidation of all mail, express, and passenger business on the Central Route. It provided that the Central Overland California & Pike's Peak Express Company should operate the line between the Missouri River and Salt Lake City, for which it would receive $470,000 per year. The Overland Mail Company would perform a like service from that city to Placerville, California. Each would pay one half the cost of transporting the "heavy mail" by sea.

Receipts from through-passengers and express and the Pony Express were to be divided equally between them, with each paying expenses on its own end of the line. Another clause provided that the Overland Mail Company should have the right to make an exclusive contract with Wells, Fargo & Company to handle all express going east from any point west of Salt Lake City and all business originating in the east going west of that point. Still another clause provided that the Overland Mail Company would appoint a general superintendent who should have charge of the whole line, but would not interfere with the details of management east of Salt Lake City.

Since the bill stipulated mail service to Denver, Colorado, three times a week, Russell and Dinsmore made a contract with E. S. Alford, Superintendent of the Western Stage Company, under which it ceased operating stages from that city to Fort Kearny. The Central Overland California & Pike's Peak Express Company's stages, which were running regularly between Denver and the Missouri River, could carry the mail. As consideration the

Western Stage Company was to receive $20,000 per year, 70% of which was paid by the Central Overland California & Pike's Peak Express Company. This contract cleared the route to Denver of all competition and gave the two companies a monopoly on all mail, express, and passenger business west of the Missouri River.

Four days after signing these contracts Russell forwarded

Courtesy of Los Angeles County Museum

copies of them to Waddell. "Believing them to be all the Co. could ask and as much as I ever encouraged them to hope for, and with all an A No. 1 contract, I am content," he said. "We should get the thing up right, work it with energy, and with its results entirely relieve R. M. and . . ."

In view of the fact that the Overland Mail Company was not, according to the stipulations of the bill passed by Congress, obliged to share its great contract with the Central Overland California & Pike's Peak Express Company it was indeed an A No. 1 contract.

Rumfield said that the contract between Russell and Dinsmore was "regarded as very advantageous to the Overland Company." This was no doubt due to several things, among them depredations along the line in Texas, seizure of horses and mules by both

Federal and Confederate forces, a falling off of express and passenger business, and above all, the grim certainty of Civil War.

While these things were happening, and preparation for the change over was being made, William H. Russell appointed Wells, Fargo & Company temporary agent for the Central Overland California & Pike's Peak Express Company in San Francisco. The transfer of the office was made on April 15, 1861, and the public instructed by means of an advertisement to deliver and receive Pony Express letters at the Wells Fargo office at California and Montgomery Street. Obviously, this appointment would expire on July 1 when the Overland Mail Company took over the western half of the line from Salt Lake City to Placerville. It should be noted that this appointment applied only to the San Francisco office and is not to be considered as "taking over" the management of any part of the route itself. That work was carried on as usual by the Division Superintendent and other employees of the Central Overland & Pike's Peak Express Company.

Since the bill and contract with the Post Office Department designated Placerville as the western terminus of the line, the Overland Mail Company had no authority to make arrangements of any kind from that place to Sacramento and San Francisco. Consequently someone, probably the postmaster at the latter city made a contract with the Pioneer Stage Line to carry the mail between Placerville and Sacramento. From there it went on to San Francisco by boat. The Overland Mail Company also turned over express packages and passengers to that line for the remainder of their journey.

The above bill and contract, in making Placerville the western terminus, actually abolished the Pony Express from that town to Sacramento, a distance of forty-nine miles, as of July 1, 1861. There was really no need for it, because the Pioneer Stage Line ran daily coaches over that stretch of road.

Wells, Fargo & Company, however, decided that it would start a Pony Express of its own over that road. This decision was announced in an advertisement in the San Francisco newspapers on June 26, 1861. It read:

". . . commencing July 1, 1861, Messrs. Wells, Fargo & Co. will run a Pony Express between San Francisco and Placerville regularly on Wednesday and Saturday of each week . . . connecting with the Overland Mail Company's Pony Express at Placerville."

It was understood, of course, that letters would go from San Francisco to Sacramento by boat.

This short line was strictly a private enterprise, with which neither the government, Overland Mail Company, nor the Central Overland California & Pike's Peak Express Company had anything to do. That being true, it would have no place in this story were it not for the fact it has been made, in part, the basis for false assumptions, misrepresentations, and undocumented claims as shown further on. It was probably started with the idea of extending the line on to Virginia City and perhaps farther, which was done later. All that, however, is not a part of our story. It should be remembered that this short line was not a segment of the original Pony Express, which ended at Placerville after July 1, 1861, and that the company which operated it never had anything to do with the operation of the line between Placerville and Salt Lake City.

In recent times much confusion and misunderstanding concerning the relationship of Wells, Fargo & Compay to the original Pony Express in 1861 and afterward, has been created by writers, reporters, publicity agents, and motion picture producers to whom historical accuracy does not seem important. Officially it had none, save as agent in San Francisco for about ten weeks from April 15 to July 1.

It has been said, and widely believed, that Wells, Fargo & Company operated the Pony Express from Sacramento to Salt Lake City during the last one third of its existence. It did nothing of the kind. That job was done by the Overland Mail Company in accordance with the contract between Russell and Dinsmore.

The vague, general statement that Wells, Fargo & Company "interests" took over the western half of the Pony Express on July 1, 1861, is also made. By this is meant, of course, the Overland Mail Company, which was formed by the Adams, American, National, and Wells, Fargo Express Companies for the purpose of carrying the mail to California in 1857 over the Southern Route. If that claim is justifiable, then the same degree of credit and consideration must be given the other three companies. Moreover, if the "interests" claim is admitted, then all four companies must be equally credited with not only operating the Pony Express on the western half of the line, but also for the stage coach, express, and passenger business on the same route. Once embarked upon this line of reasoning, it is impossible to stop short of laying claim to credit for the whole line from Placerville to St. Joseph, for the Central Overland California & Pike's Peak Express Company remained in business because of the contract between Russell and Dinsmore. Support for this argument is so frail, so lacking in actual historical qualities, so obviously exaggerated that one wonders how anyone possessed of loyalty to historical truth could predicate general conclusions and sweeping statements upon it.

It is most unfortunate that after a lapse of almost a century, unfounded statements and false claims regarding the origin, management, and ownership of the Pony Express should be bandied freely about to the detriment of those daring, energetic men who founded and operated it. To do this reflects no honor upon those involved in it. These unfounded statements and false claims have been so frequent in recent years, and the name Wells, Fargo & Company so prominently associated with it that the names of William H. Russell, Alexander Majors, and William B. Waddell are rapidly fading from the picture. This is not as it should be.

The removal of the Overland Mail Company to the Central Route was not lacking in advantages to Russell and the Central Overland California & Pike's Peak Express Company. Under the contract, Dinsmore got that portion of the route which presented the greatest difficulties and paid the least profit. Indians had harassed it more or less almost from the beginning, and it lay through the most dreary, sparsely populated region on the Continent. When viewed from this angle, Russell got much the better of the bargain. His liabilities were materially reduced, his chances for profit multiplied, and with a backlog of $470,000 per year as payment for carrying the mail, his prospects were decidedly improved.

Having worked out the contract with the Overland Mail Company Russell left Washington for home the later part of March, 1861. If he ever visited that city again there is no known record of it. He had been away about ten months, much had happened, ex-

Stage coach cover from author's collection.

planation of many things was due his partners, strained personal relations needed repairing, and the future had to be considered.

One of the items on his agenda of appointments was a meeting of the Central Overland California & Pike's Peak Express Company's Board of Directors on April 26. It had been almost a year since there had been one and many important matters demanded attention. Without a doubt many serious, perhaps painful conversations were held between him and his partners prior to that date.

When the Board met, Russell again tendered his resignation, probably by prearrangement. This time it was accepted, and Bela M. Hughes, a resident of St. Joseph, former agent for Russell, Majors & Waddell, and a personal friend of all, was elected in his stead. Although Russell retained his seat upon the Board, he was relieved of all administrative responsibilities.

One of the first problems the new president undertook to solve, with Russell's unofficial help, was that of a new route from Julesburg via Denver to Salt Lake City. The gold discoveries had proved their worth; numerous towns had been founded; Denver had grown in importance, and there was no question but that broad development of the Rocky Mountain region was assured. Therefore the people there, being no longer content with a branch mail and express line, demanded that the main route to Salt Lake City run through their country.

Early in May, 1861, Hughes and Russell arrived in Denver for the purpose of laying out that route. So far as the record goes this was the latter's first trip across the plains. They organized an exploring expedition, enlisted Jim Bridger as guide, and found a route that seemed adapted to their purposes.

In the meantime the deadline for the changeover on the Central Route was drawing near. Since it had to be completed by

Courtesy of Library, State Historical Society
of Colorado

Robert J. Spotswood

July 1, all thought of putting the new line into operation by that date was abandoned. It was never used.

Russell's trip to the Rocky Mountains fired him with belated enthusiasm for it. Had he listened to R. B. Bradford a year or two before, much of his story might have been different. With old-time zeal he feverishly set to work to repair his broken fortunes. He organized town companies, toll roads, the Colorado & Pacific Wagon, Telegraph, & Railroad Company, and became a partner in numerous mining ventures.

Although Russell was certain business on the Eastern Division under the new arragement would prove to be a bonanza for the Central Overland California & Pike's Peak Express Company, it did not turn out that way. Somebody made an "Estimate of Disbursements and Receipts" from May 1, 1861 to July 1, 1862, and sent it to Waddell. He looked it over with some skepticism no doubt, and tucked it away in his files. There it lay for eighty years without seeing the light of day.

This "Estimate" showed receipts from mail service of $476,000, which was the Eastern Division's share in the $1,000,000 subsidy from the Post Office Department. It also showed receipts for passenger service $249,600; for express, $104,000; and for Pony Express $100,000. The grand total was $929,600. Without a doubt the three last items were greatly overestimated.

The new plan went into effect but it failed to remedy the financial condition of the Central Overland California & Pike's Peak Express Company. On July 5 the Board of Directors authorized President Hughes to give a note and deed of trust upon the company and all its property to Benjamin Holladay. For some reason this was postponed until November 22 when Hughes and John W. Russell gave him a bond in the amount of $400,000 and a mortgage on the company to run for three years. In the meantime he would underwrite the company's obligation by honoring drafts, bills of exchange, acceptances etc., and advance money as needed, providing the total amount did not exceed $300,000. On the same day the company made a deed of trust with Holladay as beneficiary.

Less than three months later Holladay declared the bond forfeited and requested the trustees to sell the company. He has been accused of "freezing" the company out of business but it is extremely doubtful that he did. The trustees advertised the company for sale at auction but were enjoined from selling it. On February 15, 1862, it was again advertised for sale, and on March 7 Holladay bid it in for $100,000. He said it owed him $208,000 and that he paid claims for grain, forage, provisions, and wages to employees to the amount of $500,000. He appointed Bela M. Hughes counsel for the company and continued to operate under its charter until 1866.

A month and two days before Holladay took over the Central Overland California & Pike's Peak Express Company the telegraph line was completed and the Pony Express officially came to an end. It appears, however, that a few more runs were made, possibly to clear the route of *mochilas* in transit.

12

THE PONY BOWS
TO THE LIGHTNING

As SOON AS the 49ers in California had a chance to get their breath, they began to think about a number of advantages and conveniences that would enrich life in their far western domain. Among these was the telegraph. In 1851 O. E. Allen and C. Burnham projected the California State Telegraph Company. A year later Sweeney & Baugh, of the Merchant's Exchange, erected a short line from the business district of San Francisco to Telegraph Hill at the entrance of the bay. About the same time the Alta Telegraph Company, whose office was the starting point for the first Pony Express rider, was organized to build a line to the Carson River Valley by way of Auburn, Placerville, Mormon Island, and Sacramento.

The success of the first lines caused men with money to consider the telegraph as a profitable investment. After the Overland Mail line was put into operation, the Pacific & Atlantic Telegraph Company was organized to build a line over it to the east. By 1860 it had reached Los Angeles, where it halted.

In 1858 Frederick A. Bee organized the Placerville & St. Joseph Overland Telegraph Company to build a line eastward into Nevada. During the winter of 1859-60 it was completed to Carson City. There it halted for about a year. Californians had done their best to reach the East by telegraph. Beyond this point lay a broad desert waste reaching almost to Salt Lake City.

In the East interest in building a line to the Pacific Coast was keen. Hiram Sibley, president of Western Union Telegraph Company, had favored such an undertaking since the organization of his company in 1854. Since his associates did not agree with him, nothing was done. The Missouri & Western Telegraph Company, known as the "Stebbins Line," under Charles M. Stebbins, seized the initiative and extended its line from the Missouri River to Fort Kearny in 1860. There the Pony Express riders picked up telegrams for the West Coast and carried them to Carson City.

There is no doubt that the fleet ponies shuttling back and forth on their regular runs had much to do with crystalizing sentiment in favor of closing the long gap between the eastern and western telegraph stations. The very fact that they covered it caused people to demand a more rapid means of doing so. Private capital had done its best by building the lines up to the very threshold of civilization at both ends. Help from another source would have to be secured.

A little over two months after the Pony Express started, Congress passed a bill providing that help in the form of a subsidy of $40,000 per year for ten years to the company bridging that gap. A quarter section of land every fifteen miles and the right to take poles and other construction material from public lands was also granted. Bids for building it were to be submitted to the Secretary of Treasury.

Among the bidders was Benjamin F. Ficklin, recently ousted from his position as Route Superintendent of the Central Overland California & Pike's Peak Express Company. His bid included running a Pony Express between wire ends at regular telegraph rates after the first 600 miles were completed.

Early in October, 1860, it was announced that Hiram Sibley was the successful bidder. Apparently no route was specified, for Edward Creighton was sent to examine one along the Overland Mail line, by way of Fort Smith and Memphis. This was probably with the idea of building along that line and connecting with the Pacific & Atlantic Company at Los Angeles.

But the Southern Route was not chosen for a number of reasons. The lowering clouds of Civil War, and the certainty that the Confederacy would seize the line in its event, was one of them. Another was the fact that Northern men held the contract and Northern capital was involved in it. Still another was the fact that the Pony Express was already running regularly on

Courtesy of C.B. & Q. R.R.

Type of locomotive that pulled first Pony Express mail, April 3, 1860.

the Central Route and carrying telegrams between wire ends twice a week.

The plan, as worked out by Sibley, was to build simultaneously from both eastern and western ends. This involved consolidation of companies in California and the creation of a new one in the Middle West. To accomplish the first purpose Jeptha H. Wade was sent to the West Coast by sea in the fall of 1860. Under his direction the Placerville & St. Joseph Overland Telegraph Company, the Northern Telegraph Company, and the Pacific & Atlantic Telegraph Company were merged into the California State Telegraph Company, whose business it was to build the line from Carson Valley to Salt Lake City.

While Wade was on his long journey to the West Coast, Creighton, in company with W. R. Stebbins, was making a survey of the Central Route from Fort Kearney to Salt Lake City. They went carefully over the ground and made contracts for building the line as far as Julesburg when spring came on.

Back on the Missouri River other plans moved forward apace.

The Pacific Telegraph Company was incorporated by the Nebraska Legislature in the spring of 1861 and organized in Rochester, New York, on April 17. Among its incorporators were Hiram Sibley, Jeptha H. Wade, Charles M. Stebbins, Edward Creighton, and Benjamin F. Flickin. Wade was made President, Sibley Vice President, and Creighton General Agent and Superintendent of Construction.

Construction on the west end under James Gamble began at Fort Churchill when the first pole was set on May 27, 1861. The initial crew consisted of fifty men, twenty-six wagons, and 228 oxen. Specifications called for twenty-five poles to the mile. Two months later the line extended one hundred twenty-five miles to the east.

On July 4, of the same year, Creighton set his first pole in Omaha, Nebraska. Almost 1,000 oxen were required to haul the material and supplies for the crews working westward. By the end of August the western end of the line was at Julesburg.

In order to speed construction and create a healthy rivalry between the crews working at both ends of the line, it was agreed that the company reaching Salt Lake City first should retain the full payment for messages between the Missouri River and San Francisco until the line was completed. In addition, the loser was to pay the winner fifty dollars per day until the job was done. The Pacific Telegraph Company received sixty per cent of the government subsidy and the Overland Telegraph Company forty per cent. Pony Express riders making their semi-weekly runs not only carried telegrams between terminals but also kept each of the crews up to date on the progress of its competitor.

On both ends of the line a large construction organization had to be maintained. In the west, wire and insulators had to be brought from the Atlantic Coast around Cape Horn, then hauled on ox wagons out on the line all the way to Salt Lake City. On the eastern end they had to be transported in the same manner from the Missouri River.

But that was not all. Crews of pole cutters had to be maintained in the hills and mountains and wagon trains to haul them out to end of wire. Provisions and supplies for the crews had to be hauled from Sacramento in the west and Omaha in the east.

It has often been said that as the wire ends advanced the Pony Express riders ran only between them. This is entirely incorrect. They carried mail from St. Joseph to Sacramento, and vice versa,

Courtesy of Scott's Bluff National Monument

"The Talking Wires"

from beginning to end. They did, however, carry telegrams only between terminals.

Both Gamble and Creighton put crews to work building lines from Salt Lake City. Movement westward was under James Street, who set his first pole in that city on July 11, 1861. Creighton's men arrived in Salt Lake City on October 20, thereby winning the prize. Gamble's crew got in on the 24th. The wires were joined, and the job was done. In three months and twenty days the gap between East and West was bridged with a slender wire.

The Pony Express was fast for its day, but the electric telegraph was faster. Horseflesh could not compete with the lightning. Officially, the Pony Express ended its career on October 26, 1861, although it was not until November that the last mail was received in San Francisco over it. No doubt this was due to clearing the line of all *mochilas* in transit.

The Pony's brief hour of glory was over. For eighteen months he deservedly held the spotlight of public interest and acclaim. During that time he made three hundred eight runs each way; raced a total of 616,000 miles, a distance equal to twenty-four times around the earth; carried about 34,753 pieces of mail, and lost only one *mochila*. Of that number going east, 18,456 originated in San Francisco, and 4,900 in Sacramento. At the same time San Francisco received 9,553 from the east and Sacramento 1,844.

From these figures it is seen that the people of California supplied approximately one half of the total receipts of the Pony Express. Had the East done as well, a different story would have been told. Nobody knows what it cost the Central Overland California & Pike's Peak Express Company to equip, maintain, and operate the Pony Express, but it must have been at least $500,000. The absence of company records makes a break-down of items actually chargeable to it impossible, and the few random statements concerning it throw little light upon it. The complex activities of the company, which was also engaged in the stagecoach, express, and mail business presents additional difficulties. Alexander Majors, in his book *Seventy Years on the Frontier*, simply says the loss on the Pony Express was "several hundred thousand dollars."

Because of the high carrying charges, the Pony Express was not a popular method of transporting mail from Eastern business men and the public. Two thirds of what was placed in the *mochilas* was sent by newspapers. It is said that those of St. Louis alone paid about $100 per week in fees. Neither was it used to any great extent by government Departments in Washington.

As the momentous election of 1860 approached, special arrangements for carrying the results from Fort Kearny to Fort Churchill in record time were made. Division Superintendents were notified to choose their best men and horses and do everything possible to speed the news. On November 7 a rider dashed off from Fort Kearny at 1:00 o'clock p. m. with the information that Abraham Lincoln had been elected. It arrived at Fort Churchill on the 14th at 1:00 o'clock a. m., having been on the way six and one half days.

The Pony Express failed in only one respect; it made no money. That, however, was not the fault of the men who promoted it or of the youths who faithfully carried the *mochilas* day and night over the long trail. It was not started as a money-making operation, but it might have at least paid expenses had the people of the East been as speed conscious as were their brethren in the West.

As a strategic move in a battle for rich prizes, it was a success in every way. It eliminated the moth-eaten argument that mail service over the Central Route was not possible the year round, and emphasized, as nothing else could, the slow, ponderous service over Butterfield's "Ox-bow" route.

When the crisis precipitated by secession and approaching Civil War arose in 1860-61, the Pony Express became vitally important as the most rapid means of communication between California and the East. Loyal people out there watched the first act of the awful drama unfold day by day and eagerly awaited the arrival of each pony with news from the theater of action. That long, slender line of communication, which a handful of hostile Indians might easily break any day, was their sole reliance for keeping abreast of swiftly moving events.

It is not strange, therefore, that Californians cherished the Pony Express more than did the people of the East. Their descendants understand it better and cherish it more than anyone else to this day. In this era of instant transmission of news via radio, it is difficult to visualize those far-off days when people

The beginning of the end of the Pony Express

eagerly waited eight or ten days for the next Pony Express to bring information of what was happening to their tortured, dismembered country.

The after years of Russell, Majors, and Waddell were clouded by disappointment, hardship, and obscurity. Russell's efforts to recoup his shattered fortunes in Colorado resulted in total failure. On April 1, 1865, he assigned his assets to James P. Rogers and Charles Benjamin Russell, his son, for the benefit of creditors. His liabilities were $136,903.43. Having done this he went back to New York where for a time he engaged in the brokerage business in partnership with Thomas P. Akers. Unfortunately this was not a success either.

Eventually he was reduced to doing anything he could find. He still maintained an office at 111 Broadway, but vacated the exclusive Brevoort House. His living quarters were at 176 Fifth Avenue. His old haunts knew him no more, bankers and financiers who once fawned upon him, were now too busy to even grant him an interview, and his name, once a symbol for financial wizardry, was forgotten. When in due time his health failed he was taken to the home of his daughter, Mrs. Webster M. Samuel in St. Louis. His last home was with his son, John W. in Palmyra, Missouri, where he died September 10, 1872, in his sixtieth year.

Waddell never engaged in any kind of business again. He continued to live in his spacious home at the corner of 13th and South Street in Lexington, but his life was not a happy one. The cross currents of Civil War swirled about him, one of his sons was killed defending a slave, his home was raided again and again, and to prove his loyalty he signed an oath of allegiance to the United States. Lawsuit after lawsuit was filed against him, his angry creditors impugned his integrity, land he owned was sold on the courthouse steps for taxes, and old friends turned against him. He died at the farm home of his daughter, Mrs. A. G. Williams on April 1, 1872, at sixty-five years of age and was buried at Lexington.

Majors steeled himself against the adversity which overtook him and remained in the freighting business. In 1865 he sent two wagon trains from Nebraska City to Salt Lake City and later freighted to points in Montana. In 1867 he moved his family to Salt Lake City where he engaged in grading the roadbed and furnishing ties and telegraph poles to the Union Pacific Railroad. On May 10, 1869, he was present at the ceremony of driving the gold spike which marked the completion of the transcontinental railway.

Somehow domestic trouble developed and his home was broken up. He hopefully turned to prospecting in the Utah mountains, engaged in it for several years, but without success. After 1879 he made his home at various places, including Kansas City and Denver. In the latter place "Buffalo Bill" Cody, then at the height of his fame as a showman, found him living in a little shack engaged in writing the story of his life. "Buffalo Bill" hired Prentice Ingraham to edit it and paid for having it printed under the title *Seventy Years on the Frontier*. He died in Chicago on January 14, 1900, in his eighty-sixth year, and was buried in Union Cemetery, Kansas City, Missouri.

The story of the building of the Pacific Railroad, while not necessarily an integral part of that of the Pony Express, is, like that of the overland telegraph, closely related to it. Although it had little bearing upon that instituion, as such, it did upon related activities: freighting, stage coaching, express business, and transportation of mail across the Great Plains. All of these continued under radically changed conditions for many years.

The decade, 1859-69, introduced the Golden Era of westward expansion and development. During those thrillling days the East was inseparably wedded to the West and the foundation for a truly Continental Power was laid. It was during that same period that the principle of "*one nation, indivisible*" was established through the agony of Civil War, but that is not a part of our story.

It is indeed remarkable that such a brief period of time should produce three of the most thrilling stories in Western American history: that of the Pony Express, the telegraph, and the Pacific Railroad. In a definite sense they were all born of the same fundamental need, that of communication between widely separated parts of the nation. They also had this in common, the place of their nativity was the West.

The early movement for a railroad from the Missouri River to the Pacific Coast was spearheaded by Senator Thomas Hart Benton, long time Senator from Missouri. The route he advocated began at St. Louis, crossed the state to its western boundary, and proceeded across the plains along the Central Route to San Francisco. He talked about it so much in Congress, in the newspapers, and in speeches throughout his home state that the people of Missouri became extremely railroad minded.

In 1836 a convention of fifty-nine delegates to consider the matter was held in St. Louis. A year later Governor L. W. Boggs requested the legislature to memorialize Congress on the subject. An index to the prevailing interest in it is seen in the fact that no less than seventeen railroads, with a combined capitalization of $7,875,000, on paper, were incorporated in that session.

When the Chinese ports were opened to American traders in 1844 the proposition received new impetus. This prompted Eli Whitney to petition Congress for a grant of land sixty miles wide extending from Lake Michigan to Puget Sound. Since the route lay wholly within Northern Territory, Southern legislators were opposed to it. Another item to which they objected was the amount of land requested as a subsidy.

The acquisition of California as the result of the War with Mexico immeasurably strengthened the railroad movement and assured its ultimate success. The people of that far western territory, of the North, and of Missouri, insisted that the line, if built, should follow the Central Route. Of course, those of the South were equally insistent that it should run over the Southern Route.

Since the eastern end of the line along the Central Route would cross various towns in Missouri, among them Lexington, there began the dream of railroad centers. Having risen to a position of civic importance and influence, William H. Russell took great interest in the proposition. He helped organize the Lexington & Boonville Railroad Company in 1853, the Lexington & Davies County Railroad Company in 1854, and became a director in each.

When Russell, Majors & Waddell organized in 1854 with head-quarters at Leavenworth, his interest in railroads was broadened. He helped organize the Leavenworth, Pawnee & Western Rail-road Company and when it was chartered became a director in it. The road was authorized to build a line from Leavenworth to the western boundary of the Territory, which at that time was the Continental Divide of the Rocky Mountains. In 1857 $156,000 worth of stock was subscribed and construction begun. The great railroad bill of 1862 granted this company five sections of land per mile along its route. The following year it was acquired by the Union Pacific, Eastern Division. It was while this line was being built across Kansas that young William Frederick Cody earned his title "Buffalo Bill."

Both Russell and his partners knew full well that the laying of steel rails along the Central Route would put their stage-coaches and Conestogas out of business. When Major M. Jeff Thompson swung the first *mochila* into place at St. Joseph on April 3, 1860, he prophesied that the dust raised by the flying pony would hardly settle to earth before the steam of the loco-motive would be seen upon the horizon. Majors declared that the "tireless iron horse" would, ere long, supersede those of flesh and blood. Russell appears to have said nothing about it, but if he had he certainly would have echoed the same sentiments.

The Pacific Railway Bill of 1862, which transmuted the dream of binding the nation together with steel rails reaching from the Missouri River to the Pacific Coast, was passed and signed by President Lincoln on July 1. The road it authorized was to be built from both ends and by two companies. Each was given a right of way four hundred feet wide and allowed to take building material, timber, stone, or whatever was needed and available from public lands. For every mile of track laid, they would receive ten sections of land and were permitted to borrow government bonds to the amount of $16,000 per mile in level country, $32,000 in the foothills of the Rocky and Sierra Nevada Mountains, and $48,000 in the mountains. If the line was not completed by 1876 it was to be forfeited to the government;

if it were, the companies had the privilege of repaying the government bonds out of future earnings.

California's first railroad was the Sacramento & Folsom, twenty-three miles long, which was completed in 1856. While it served only a tiny fragment of the great state, it kept alive the hopes of the people for rail communication with the East. The vice president of this infant road was Captain William Tecumseh Sherman who later won fame for his march from Atlanta to the sea.

Fourteen months after the Pony Express was started, the Central Pacific Railroad Company was incorporated on June 28, 1861. Perhaps the real father of it was Theodore D. Judah, who built the Sacramento & Folsom road. Certainly he was the first man with practical railroad building experience to advocate it. He took his plan to Congress on several occasions, made preliminary surveys over the Sierras, and received a small amount of financial support from a number of mountain towns. As usual where men of vision are concerned, he was branded as a money-grabber and his scheme fantastic.

Judah's conviction that the road could be built and his flaming enthusiasm for it finally caught the attention of four men in San Francisco. They were Leland Stanford, grocery man; Charles Crocker, who ran a dry goods store; Collis P. Huntington and Mark Hopkins, dealers in hardware. Of these Stanford became the master organizer and political leader, Huntington and Hopkins financial geniuses, and Crocker an able construction engineer whose feats aroused the admiration of builders throughout the world.

Stanford was elected president, Huntington vice president, Hopkins treasurer, and Crocker one of the directors. Judah again went to Washington, where he played an important part in the passage of the Railroad Bill, while Huntington went to New York to raise money. Judah was successful, but Huntington met with a cool reception. Men with money regarded the enterprise as extremely risky and the hope of financial return too slim. The length of the railroad would be approximately 2,000 miles, most of which was through an unsettled wilderness. Much of it was desert and known to be fruitful only in spots. Moreover, between the Eastern and Western terminals lay two of the most rugged mountain ranges in the world. Besides, the country was cut in twain and Civil War was raging. Small wonder then that men of wealth viewed the proposition with jaundiced eyes. The officers of the company were aware of all this but their determination never faltered. When the Railroad Bill was passed and signed, Huntington wired his associates, "We have drawn the elephant, now let us see if we can harness him."

Although Eastern capitalists were not interested in the railroad as an investment, they were impressed with the credit rating of the "Big Four", as the San Francisco merchants were known. When they offered to personally guarantee the interest on a limited amount of Central Pacific bonds, enough money to start construction was forthcoming.

The job ahead was the greatest, most difficult ever undertaken in railroad history. All of the rolling stock, steel, and other equipment had to be brought from the Atlantic Coast around Cape Horn, a voyage of eight to ten months. At one time the company had thirty vessels on the high seas loaded with material and machinery. Provisions for the workers had to be brought to California via sea also, vast quantities of them from China and other Asiatic countries.

After a short distance of comparatively easy building on level ground, the roadbed leaped upward to a height of 7,000 feet in the space of a few miles. Picks, shovels, wheelbarrows, and one-horse carts were the only aids to grading in those days. Dynamite had not yet come into general use, and the only reliance for blasting away the granite walls of the Sierras was ordinary black powder. The job confronting them was literally one of hand carving.

In those days nothing was more scarce in California than white laborers. Good wages were paid in the mines; agriculture was developing, and men just did not take to the idea of building a railroad over the mountains with pick and shovel. At one time Crocker brought out two thousand laborers from San Francisco and put them to work. Within a few days only about a hundred were still on the job.

One day Crocker suggested the idea of employing Chinese coolies to do the work. J. H. Strobridge, superintendent of construction, opposed it. Crocker insisted that the race which had built the great Chinese Wall by hand could also build the Central Pacific Railroad. Strobridge finally consented to try fifty coolies. They did so well that fifty more were employed. Then more, and more, as their value was proved. Before the road was finished, 12 to 15,000 were on the payroll. Clipper ships brought their food from China, and when it was seen that a native doctor was needed, Dr. C. T. Yee, an herbalist, was brought over to care for them. Today the Southern Pacific owes a heavy debt of gratitude to those humble Chinese coolies, for they actually built most of it from Sacramento to Promontory Point, Utah.

The first rail was laid in Sacramento October 26, 1863. Two years later rail-end had reached Colfax, fifty-five miles away. By the end of 1865 the battle to carry the road over the Sierras was on in real earnest. To cross the summit a tunnel 1,659 feet long was necessary. It was decided to work it from four faces. To do this it was necessary to sink a shaft at the summit. This was driven downward through solid rock so hard that sometimes they could make only seven inches a day. A hoisting engine was dismantled and the boiler moved up the trail to the mouth of the shaft by ten yoke of oxen.

The work was begun early in 1866, and by December of that year the shaft was deep enough to begin the laterals. A year of hard work was required to complete the tunnel from this point. To cross the Sierras, fifteen tunnels of varying length were necessary. During the winter months snow in the cuts and slides down the sides of mountains presented such a hazard that thirty-seven miles of snow-sheds had to be constructed. Into these went 65,000,000 feet of lumber and 900 tons of bolts and spikes. They cost more than $2,000,000.

During the winter of 1866-67 three locomotives, forty cars, and material for forty miles of track were hauled along the trail to Truckee River Canyon where light snowfalls made grading and building possible at that time of year. On December 13, 1867, the first of these locomotives poked its nose over the California-Nevada line, but there remained seven difficult miles to build in the Sierras. When these were completed they were free of those difficulties encountered in the mountains.

Early in 1869 word came that the Union Pacific's "Irish Terriers," as the track layers were called, laid six miles of track in one day. Crocker's Chinese coolies promptly laid seven. The Union Pacific bettered it and Crocker boasted his men could lay ten miles in one day and was willing to wager $10,000 it could be done. Thomas C. Durant promptly covered it.

In preparation for the test, ties were scattered along the right of way several miles in advance; other material was placed at strategic points, and everything planned with military precision. In the presence of officials of both companies, including General G. M. Dodge, chief engineer of construction for the Union Pacific, newspaper correspondents, and visitors, the work started on the morning of April 28, 1869. When the twelve hour day was over they had laid ten miles and fifty-six feet of track. This feat brought them within a few miles of Promontory Point, the designated place for the meeting of the lines.

The Union Pacific Railroad Company was organized June 27, 1863, with W. B. Ogden as president, Thomas C. Durant vice president, and General Grenville M. Dodge chief engineer. The following winter, ground was broken and a bit of grading done at Omaha, Nebraska, the eastern terminal. There the matter rested for more than six months. The first rail was laid in July, 1865.

Although the eastern portion of the road lay through level prairie country the overall difficulties facing its builders were tremendous. There being no railroad connection at Omaha at that time, all material, machinery, locomotives, men, and cars had to be brought up the Missouri River from St. Louis by boat. Ties also had to be brought over long distances, with the result that until the road reached a part of the country where they were available closer at hand, they cost the company on the average of $2.50 each.

By January 1866 thirty miles of track had been laid and by the end of the year the line had advanced 260 additional miles half way across the State of Nebraska. The following year the laying of 200 more miles brought it to the summit of the Rocky Mountains between Cheyenne and Laramie, Wyoming.

This road, like the Central Pacific, was literally built by hand. Horse or mule drawn scrapers, dump carts, picks, and shovels were the only tools they had. The workman were mostly ex-soldiers, Federal and Confederate, who after four years of war welcomed this opportunity to earn a livelihood in a peaceful occupation. They were accustomed to living in camps, and when the line reached Indian country were formed into companies, battalions, and regiments under officers who had well-earned military titles. They were armed with rifles, which they carried to the job and stacked within easy reach. On many occasions they dropped their picks and shovels, seized their guns, and successfully repelled an Indian attack.

The Red Men, being fully aware that the building of the road through the heart of their country meant their doom, violently opposed it. In desperation they marshalled their forces and offered what resistance they could. So continuous were their attacks upon the surveyors, graders, and track layers that before the line was half way across Nebraska it became necessary to send soldiers along the line to guard the workmen. Oakes Ames said, "Their troops guarded us, and we reconnoitered, surveyed, located, and built inside of their picket line."

The achievement for 1868 was 425 miles through the roughest portion of the route. Despite this fact they now enjoyed an advantage they had not hitherto possessed. Ties, telegraph poles, and stone for building purposes were to be obtained close at hand. They also had the advantage of securing provisions and other supplies from the Mormons in Utah.

The building of 125 miles in 1869 brought them to Promontory Point in the desert country of Utah where a colorful ceremony on May 10 of that year marked the joining of the rails of the two companies. The epic task was finished and one might now travel in comfort from the Atlantic Coast to the Golden Gate.

The crowd at Promontory Point that momentous day numbered only 500 or 600 people. President Stanford of the Central Pacific brought a small party from the West Coast on a special train. Another on the Union Pacific bore Vice President Thomas C. Durant, Sidney Dillon, chairman of the Board of Directors, and General Grenville M. Dodge. From Camp Douglas came a contingent of soldiers and a military band. Salt Lake City's Tenth Ward band, with $1,200 worth of new instruments recently received from London, was also there. In addition there were workmen from both roads, a number of newspaper correspondents, and a few spectators. Among the latter was Alexander Majors and his youngest son Benjamin who perhaps understood the significance of it all better than anyone else. While others celebrated the beginning of a new, glorious era, he mourned the passing of those fabulous days in which he had played a conspicuous part.

"My calling," he sadly remarked years later, "as a freighter and overland stager having been deposed by the building of the telegraph lines and the completion of the transcontinental railway, I was compelled to look for a new industry."

The main portion of the ceremony was devoted to the driving of a golden spike into a beautifully finished tie of California laurel wood eight feet long, eight inches wide, six inches thick, and bound with silver. In order that the whole nation might share in this part of the important event, a Western Union telegraph wire had been run from the top of the nearest pole to a little table beside the spot where the laurel tie was to be put in.

When it had been properly placed by J. H. Strobridge of the Central Pacific and S. B. Reed of the Union Pacific, President Stanford stepped forward, took up a silver-headed maul, made cumbersome by telegraph wires attached to it, swung at the golden spike—*and missed it!* He then handed the maul to Durant, who out of consideration for Stanford also missed. Following

Pony Express Statue, St. Joseph, Missouri, eastern terminus of famed mail route.

him, various guests were invited to tap it. Was Alexander Majors one of these? Probably not, but it would have been appropriate for him to have tapped out a dirge for the days gone beyond recall.

Nationwide interest in the event marking the completion of the steel road to the Pacific Coast was keen. In Chicago a great, impromptu celebration was staged in the streets, a crowd gathered in Buffalo to hear the telegraph signals, sang *The Star Spangled Banner* and listened to speeches. Bells were rung and cannons fired in Philadelphia. In New York, Trinity Church was thrown open at midday and a large number of people assembled to hear an address by the Reverend Doctor Vinton.

The completion of the transcontinental railroad ushered in the most remarkable era of development of national resources, advance of civilization, and spread of population the world ever saw. It should be remembered, however, that the emigrant trains

SITE OF
OLD PLATTE BRIDGE
BUILT BY
LOUIS GUINARD
1858—59

IMMEDIATELY SOUTH AND
WEST ARE THE SITES OF
PLATTE BRIDGE STATION.
FIRST OVERLAND TELE-
GRAPH, STAGE, AND PONY
EXPRESS STATIONS ON
THE OLD OREGON TRAIL.

ERECTED BY
NATRONA COUNTY
HISTORICAL SOCIETY
JULY 26, 1930

Platte Bridge Monument located at present Casper, Wyoming, at what was
known as the "Mormon Ferry." It was a time-saver to both Pony Express riders
and other travelers on the Oregon Trail, in that it eliminated ferrying across
the Platte River.

plodding their weary westward way along the dusty trails, the freighter's Conestogas, the romantic stagecoach, the Pony Express, and the telegraph constituted stepping-stones leading in that direction. The traveler speeding over the old trails on a stream-lined train at ninety miles an hour or looking down upon them from the stratosphere may not be aware of what happened along them a century and a quarter ago. If he is informed, however, he will probably undertake to visualize the weeks and months of slow, toilsome travel necessary to cover the same ground, the risk of starvation, danger of attack by merciless savages, burning thirst, sickness, deaths along the way, heat of summer, and cold of winter, which were stern realities to those who traveled them in bygone days.

Long since the Pony Express saga won for itself a secure, permanent place in the catalogue of American Folklore. Better than any other perhaps, it breathes the spirit of American ingenuity, resourcefulness and daring. Best of all, it is a record of youthful courage, endurance, and loyalty to a given task.

The young men who rode the racing ponies, mere boys in their latter 'teens many of them, were of a type and quality who deserve the unqualified admiration of youth the world over. They were clean, God-fearing, worthy of trust, and modest in the extreme. When the "Great Adventure" was over they slipped away, most of them into oblivion, with no thought other than that they had done their work well.

Today the Pony Express is a memory, but what a memory it is! Already the rider is enshrined in the nation's Hall of Heroes along with Captain John Smith, Daniel Boone, Kit Carson, Jedediah S. Smith, Francis X. Aubrey and other notables. Fortunate indeed is a people who possesses a story like this with which to enthrall and inspire its youth.

BIBLIOGRAPHY

For the sake of brevity, and to avoid repetition, the limited bibliography listed below covers only that portion of the story relating to the Pony Express. That for collateral, background material, such as the biographies of the members of the firm of Russell, Majors & Waddell; the Leavenworth & Pike's Peak Express Company; the Central Overland California & Pike's Peak Express Company; financial matters, bond incident, etc. will be found in full in the authors' *Empire on Wheels*.

A

Adams, James Truslow, *Album of American History*, (New York, 1946), 3 volumes.
Alta California, April 3, 4, 1860.
Aull, James and Robert, *Letter Books* ii, iii, v, Lexington Missouri Historical Society—MS.
Aull, James and Robert, *Order Book* v. MS.

B

Bangs, Oliver, *Bounty Land Warrant No. 7848-160-1812*, in Bangs File, Records of Veteran's Administration, National Archives, Washington, D.C.—MS. Copy in authors' library.
Bangs, Oliver, *Letter to Mr. Haswell*, Aug. 24, 1816. In Bangs File, Records of Veteran's Administration, National Archives, Washington, D.C.—MS. Copy in authors' library.
Bangs, Oliver, *Notes on*, in Bangs File, Records of Veteran's Administration, National Archives, Washington, D.C.—MS. Copy in authors' library.
Bancroft, Hubert Howe, *History of Nevada, Colorado, and Wyoming* (San Francisco, 1890).
Bancroft, Hubert Howe, *History of Oregon* (San Francisco, 1886).
Boder, Bartlett, "The Pony Express" in *Museum Graphic* ii, 4-7.
Bradley, Glen D., *The Pony Express* (Chicago, 1913).
Book of Original Entries, Lafayette County, Missouri.
Burton, Sir Richard F., *The City of the Saints* (New York, 1927).

C

Carter, Kate B., *Riders of the Pony Express* (Salt Lake City, 1947).
Case, Theodore S., *History of Kansas City* (1888).
Chapman, Arthur, *The Pony Express* (New York, 1932).
Clampitt, John W., *Echoes From the Rocky Mountains* (New York, 1880).

Collins, Allan C., *Story of America in Pictures* (New York, 1935).

Contract, between William H. Russell, representing the Central Overland California & Pike's Peak Express Company, and William B. Dinsmore, representing the Overland Mail Company, March 16, 1861. Copy in authors' library.

Conkling, Roscoe P. and Margaret Conkling, *The Butterfield Overland Mail Company* (Glendale) two volumes.

Cushing, Marshall, *The Story of Our Post Office* (Boston, 1893).

D

Darby, Ada Clair, Emily Stuber, and Mrs. I. R. Bundy, *Report to Pony Express Celebration Committee*, St Joseph, Missouri, 1923 — MS. Copy in authors' library.

Deseret News, April 11, 1860.

Dick, Everett, *Vanguards of the Frontier* (New York, 1914).

Dictionary of American Biography (New York, 1933, xvi).

Driggs, Howard R., *The Pony Express Goes Through* (New York, 1935).

E

Egan, William M., *Pioneering the West, 1846-1878* (Richmond, Utah, 1917).

Ellenbecker, John G., *The Pony Express* (Marysville, n. d.).

Estimate of Disbursements and Receipts, May 1, 1861 to July 1, 1862. MS. Copy in authors' library.

F

First Baptist Church, Lexington, Missouri, *Minutes*, May 20, 1840.

Fisher, Dr. Ray H., "The Pony Express," in *Improvement Era*, Feb., 1949.

Forsyth, Brigadier General George A., *The Soldier*, vol. ii in *Builders of the Nation* (New York, 1900).

Forsyth, Brigadier General George A., "A Frontier Fight," in *Harper's New Monthly Magazine*, June, 1895.

Fort Laramie National Monument, U. S. Department of the Interior, 1942.

Frederick, J. V., *Ben Holladay, The Stagecoach King* (Glendale, 1940).

Fremont, Jessie Benton, *Souvenirs of My Time* (Boston, 1887).

French, James S., *Letter to George C. Whiting*, in Bangs File, Records of Veteran's Administration, National Archives, Washington, D.C.—MS. Copy in authors' library.

G

Golder, Frank Alfred, *The March of the Mormon Battalion* (New York, 1928).
Gothenburg (Nebraska) Times, July 27, 1932.
Gove, Captain Jesse; *The Utah Expedition* (Concord, New Hampshire, 1928).

H

Hafen, Le Roy R., *The Overland Mail*, (Cleveland, Ohio, 1926).
Hagen, Olaf T., "The Pony Express Starts From St. Joseph." in *Missouri Historical Review*, xliii, 1-7.
Hanks, L. F., *Letter to authors*, July 9, 1953.
Harlow, Alvin F., *Old Post Bags* (New York, 1928).
Hauck, Louise Paltt, "The Pony Express Celebration," in *Missouri Historical Review*, xvii, 435-439.
Heitman, Francis B., *Historical Register and Dictionary of the United States Army* (Washington, 1903), vol. i.
Honnell, W. R., Willie Whitewater (Kansas City, 1950).
Howes, Cecil, "Pony Express Planned in Kansas City Edged Out by Telegraph," in *Kansas City Star*, Oct. 21, 1946.
Hungerford, Edward, *Wells Fargo* (New York, 1949).
Hunt, Elmer Munson, "Abbot-Downing and the Concord Coach," in *Historical New Hampshire*, Nov. 1945.
Hurlburt, Archer B., *Forty-Niners* (New York, 1949).

I

Inman, Colonel Henry and Colonel William F. Cody, *Great Salt Lake Trail* (Topeka, Kansas, 1914).

K

Kansas Historical Collections (Topeka, Kansas), vols. ix, xi, xii, xiii, xiv, xv, xvii.
Kansas Historical Quarterly (Topeka, Kansas), vols. ii, xii.
Kansas City Star, Jan. 15, 1900, Jan. 29, 1927.

L

Leavenworth (Kansas) Daily Times, Jan. 30, Feb. 10, 1860.
Lexington Baptist Female College, *Minutes, Board of Trustees*, June 15, 1855, in Lexington, Missouri Historical Society.
Lexington Advertiser, Oct. 13, 1845.
Lexington Express, July 4, 1840; March 28, 1848; April 26, May 31, Nov. 8, 1854; June 15, 1855.

Lexington Intelligencer, April 18, 1891.
Loeb, Julius, "The Pony Express," in *The American Philatelist*, Nov. 1930.

M

Mabey, Charles R., *The Pony Express*, (Salt Lake City 1940).
Marriage Record Book B, Lafayette County, Missouri.
Marriage Record Book No. 1, Jackson County, Missouri.
Majors, Alexander, *Seventy Years on the Frontier* (New York, 1893).
Merriam, Lucius P., "The Telegraphs of the Bond Aided Pacific Railroads," in *Political Science Quarterly*, ix, 187.
Missouri Historical Review (Columbia, Missouri), Vol. xxi.
Missouri Republican, March 28, 1860.
Morgan, Gene, *Westward the Course of Empire* (Chicago, 1945).
Morehead, Charles R., "Personal Recollections," in W. E. Connelley, *Doniphan's Expedition* (Kansas City, 1907), 600-622.
Mullins, P. A. *Biographical Sketches of Edward Creighton, et al.*, (Omaha, 1901).
Museum Graphic (St. Joseph, Missouri), vol. iii.

N

New York Herald, March 26, 1860.

O

Ormsby, Waterman, Lyle H. Wright and Josephine M. Bynum, eds., *The Butterfield Overland Mail Company* (San Marino, 1942).
Oran, "Tropical Journeyings—Panama Railroad," in *Harper's New Monthly Magazine*, Jan. 1859.
Oslin, George P., *Letter to the authors*, July 10, 1953.

P

Pack, Mary, "The Romance of the Pony Express," in *Union Pacific Magazine*, Aug. 1923.
Pioneer Nevado (Reno, Nevada) 1951.
Pony Express (Placerville, California), Feb. 1937; Nov. 1938; Jan., Oct., Nov., 1939; April, 1940; Feb., June, Nov., 1941; Oct., 1944; Sept., 1949; April, 1953.

R

Reichman, Warren N., "Ninety Years of Controversy Started with Hanging of Joseph A. Slade," in Virginia City, Montana. *Madisonian*, May 29, 1953.
Record Books, F. to M., Lafayette County, Missouri.

Remsburg, George J., "Pony Express Riders I Have Known," in *Pony Express*, Sept., Oct., Nov., Dec., 1934; Jan., Feb., March, Nov., 1935; June 1936. Photostats in authors' library.

Richardson, Albert D., *Beyond the Mississippi*, (Hartford, 1867).

Root, Frank A. and William E. Connelley, *Overland Stage to California* (Topeka, Kansas, 1901).

Root, George A. and Russell K. Hickman, "Pike's Peak Express Companies," in *Kansas Historical Quarterly*, vols. xiii and xiv.

Rumfield, Hiram S., *Letters of an Overland Mail Agent in Utah*, ed. by Archer Butler Hurlburt (Worcester, Massachusetts, 1928).

Russell, Milton C., *Letter to Authors*, July 22, 1953.

Russell Family History—MS. Copy in authors' library.

Russell, William H., Alexander Majors, and William B. Waddell, *Contract of Partnership*, Dec. 28, 1854—MS. Copy in authors' library.

Russell, William H., Alexander Majors, John S. Jones, and William B. Waddell, *Contract to take over Leavenworth & Pike's Peak Express Company*, October 28, 1859—MS. Copy in authors' library.

Russell, William H., and William B. Waddell, representing the Central Overland California & Pike's Peak Express Company, Contract with citizens of St. Joseph, Missouri, March 2, 1860—MS. Copy in authors' library.

Russell, William H., *Letter to William B. Waddell*, June 19, 1860.

S

Sacramento (California) Union, April 2, 14, 1860.

Scudder, John, "The Pony Express," in *Lexington News*, Aug. 22, 1888.

Sanford, A. B., *The Story of Bob Spottswood*—MS. In Colorado State Museum.

San Francisco Bulletin, April 3, 1860.

Settle, Raymond W., *March of the Mounted Riflemen* (Glendale, 1940).

Settle, Raymond W., and Mary Lund Settle, *Empire on Wheels* (Stanford, 1949).

Sharp, James P., "The Pony Express Stations," in *Improvement Era*, Feb., March, 1945.

Shoemaker, Floyd C., "The Pony Express—Commemoration—Stables and Museum," in *Missouri Historical Review*, xliv, 343-363.

Slayback, Mrs. Alonzo, *Genealogy of the John Waddell Family*—MS.

Southern Pacific, *Seventy-five years of Progress* (San Francisco, 1944).

Spring, Agnes Wright, *Letter to Authors*, June 7, 1953.

Stone, Irving, *Immortal Wife* (Garden City, 1946).

St. Joseph Missouri City Directory, 1860-1861.

St. Joseph (Missouri) Gazette, Aug. 29, 1923.

St. Joseph (Missouri) Weekly West, March 31, April 4, 7, 1860.

St. Joseph (Missouri) News-Press, April 11, 1938; Oct. 31, 1941, quoted in *Missouri Historical Review* xliv, 342.

Starnes, Lee, "The Pony Express Mystery," in *Museum Graphic*, iii, 4-11.

T

Thomas, India, *Letter to the Authors*, Aug. 18, 1953.

U

United States House of Representatives, 34 cong., 1 sess., *Executive Document No. 17*.

United States Senate, 31 cong., 1 sess., *Executive Document No. 1*.

United States Senate, 31 cong., 2d sess., *Executive Document No. 2*.

United States Senate, 33 cong., 2d sess., *Executive Document No. 68*.

United States Senate, 36 cong., 2d sess., *Report of Committee on Military Affairs*.

Union Pacific Magazine, August, 1923.

Union Pacific Railroad, *A Brief History* (Omaha, 1946).

V

Visscher, William Lightfoot, *A Thrilling and Truthful Account of the Pony Express, or Blazing the Westward Way* (Chicago, 1946).

W

Waddell, John I., William B. Waddell, and Robert B. Bradford, *Contract of Partnership*, April 25, 1850—MS. Copy in authors' library.

Warman, Cy., "The Railroad," in *Builders of the Nation* (New York, 1898), vol. i.

Wellman, Paul I., "The Silent Partner," in *Kansas City Star*, Nov. 22, 1942.

Winther, Oscar Osburn, *Via Western Express and Stagecoach* (Stanford, 1945).

Y

Young, William, *History of Lafayette County* (Indianapolis, 1910).